HOW TO
SURVIVE

PRISON?

HOW TO SURVIVE

PRISON?

STEVEN FAZEKAS

authorHOUSE®

AuthorHouse™
1663 Liberty Drive
Bloomington, IN 47403
www.authorhouse.com
Phone: 1-800-839-8640

First published by AuthorHouse 4/30/2010

ISBN: 978-1-4520-1451-7 (e)
ISBN: 978-1-4520-1452-4 (sc)

Library of Congress Control Number: 2010905517

Printed in the United States of America
Bloomington, Indiana

This book is printed on acid-free paper.

CONTENTS

Since this book is dedicated to Americans who have to go to prison perhaps "A Guide for Americans Going to Prison" would have been a better title. We have manuals, handbooks, references and 'do it yourself' on practically everything – with so many Americans incarcerated – it is fair to say a guide to prison is long overdue.

You may be one of those Americans who had already lost at trial or admitted guilt in a plea agreement and is now waiting to be sent to prison for the first time. You are dreading the day of your sentence; you are dreading the day when you'll actually be taken to prison. You have conjured up an image: all those movies, the TV, the newspapers, all that Hollywood. Forget about them! They are all wrong. Despite what you have seen or heard before you have no idea what's waiting for you, but you will after you read this book.

(On the other hand) you might be the one who has never been in trouble with the law and never been arrested, perhaps you never even had a parking ticket. You are not a criminal, you don't intend to be one hence you don't think you need this book. Well, you are sorely mistaken. Please hold your laugh and contempt, this is not a tongue-in-cheek statement: You yourself may need this book sooner than you can (ever) imagine.

While this book is aimed at first-timers, second time offenders could still benefit from its refreshment. Third time around and beyond guys are reading the wrong book; they should be reading the Bible since nothing else can help them.

Anyway for those who laughed at my earlier statement, for those who think (that) this book is not for them, herewith some sobering facts:

According to the U.S. Department of Justice, as of January 2005 there were 2.3 million persons incarcerated in the United States of America. Some statistics claim/predict that this number will exceed 2.5 million by the year-end of 2010. In other words 2.5 million Americans are behind bars in various state, county, federal lock-ups, jails, prisons, and penitentiaries. According to USA Today (Oct. 24, 2005) the U.S. incarceration rate was 724 per 100,000 – 25% higher than that of any other nation. In addition to this there are an approximate 5 million Americans on parole, probation, work-release, work-camp, halfway-house, boot-camp, house-arrest, ankle bracelet, community-control, juvenile detention center, drug-rehab program and so on and so on as part of their sentence mandated by the courts. This is a staggering 7.5 million people, 2.5% of the entire population. This is more than the population of some European countries; like Sweden, Denmark, Norway or Switzerland. This means that one out of every fortieth Americans, one out of every 40 persons, out of a total population of 300 million are either incarcerated or under some kind of prison or jail control. When we deduct children (aged fourteen and under) from this number we end up with an approximate population of 170 million. In this case the percentage jumps up to 4.4% meaning that every twenty-third American over the age of fourteen is locked up, or under some kind of legal supervision, which are essentially extensions of prisons.

In the same time the average percentage of incarceration for the 27 member European Union is 1.03%, in other words approximately one out of one hundred European is incarcerated. The highest incarceration rate occurs in Britain with 1.4%, in Asia the worst is Indonesia with 1.6%, in Africa Nigeria with 1.8%, in Latin America, Colombia with 1.7%, while Australia and New Zealand compares the best with a combined average of 0.9%. There is no data available for Russia and China – might as well because to equal our 2.5% incarceration rate China would have to have at least 32.5 million of its people locked up. By all account we all know that is certainly not the case.

In Europe and perhaps in the rest of the world imprisonment is incidental (or accidental). In America incarceration is part of life. Our prisons not only house criminals, some of our social problems are also behind bars. Besides punishing the guilty and incarcerating lots of innocents our justice system has evolved (developed) into an industry, and unfortunately into a very profitable industry. There are substantial forces in the United States whose vested interest keeps prisons going and growing.

If you are fortunate enough not to be part of the prison statistics surely you know someone – not so removed from yourself – who may benefit from this book. Bear in mind that sooner or later every twenty-third adult American will end up in jail or prison. It could be your friend, a friend of a friend, a relative, a family member, an acquaintance, a colleague, your boss, a fellow worker or perhaps yourself. To paraphrase Bobby Brown who perhaps intended his statement as a joke, he says that since he's been to jail, he is a real American. Sadly he may – unintentionally – have captured the essence, since sooner or later you may not be a 'true' American unless you have been to prison or jail. If you think of it, indeed more Americans served time in prison than in the armed forces. You can argue that serving time will soon be as American as apple pie and baseball. So you see you'll need this book. You can give it for birthdays, Christmas and Thanksgiving, for anniversaries, graduation or even as a retirement gift. You can buy it for friends and foes alike, you can give it as a surprise, a hint, a warning, or just simply keep it for yourself you'll never know when you will need it. Believe me I have been there done that.

Anyway this is no 'zillion little pieces', this is the real thing from beginning to end. I indeed 'been there, done that'. My credentials are 'impeccable' herewith some references:

Hungarian State Penitentiary .... ER – 0765
Miami-Dade County Jail 0389921
Department of Correction, State of Florida B02560
Bureau of Prisons, U.S. Federal Government 63927004

Dear Reader, this is not a novel. This is not the work of someone's fantasy. This is an educational literature offered to those unfortunate souls who could benefit from my experiences. So go ahead read it, one day (never say never) you may need this book's guidance.

CHAPTER 1

Mind over matter
(An introductory overview of the system you just entered.)

So you thought you would never get arrested, you thought it could never happen to you. You are either too clever or simply not a criminal. All those guys in handcuffs and behind bars you thought deserved to be there. In your mind they were all criminals or all stupid, in any case you were neither of them. But now the handcuff is on you and the sky is falling onto your head. Yes actually it is, because even if you are acquitted your world will never be the same. The world you have lived in before has gone forever and you will never get it back. You are in a different universe now with different rules and your previous world does not want you back. Now you've been given a number, once, twice, three times. Regardless if you are guilty or innocent you are a criminal. You are wondering how this could have happened to you? You did nothing wrong, you are a decent man, somebody is lying, somebody is framing you. You are innocent or perhaps you are guilty, but they don't know that. Here you are wondering who told on you? Who betrayed you? How did you get into this mess?

Anyhow guilty or innocent it no longer matters. You have already been given a number you are branded, even if you manage to wiggle out of its tentacles for a while you are now in the system forever.

After you've been cuffed you'll never be the same. Perhaps you will bond out for now and breathe with a sigh. You may not know yet that the system you just entered, for the time being pretends you are innocent. Innocent until proven guilty, nobody really believes that, perhaps not even yourself. They just set you free before your trial so the bondsman, the attorneys, the sheriff and the court all can make money on you. You are out on bond but everybody looks at you with a difference. You are a suspicious person in everyone's eyes. You may be guilty or at best you are not a hundred percent innocent. Your friends, your co-workers even your family start treating you differently. Their minds have been poisoned although they do their best to hide their feelings. Can you blame them? You used to be like them. You have believed the mantra that our justice system is infallible that they would never arrest an innocent man. Even if someone got acquitted, you always have taken it with a grain of salt. "Well, he must have had a good lawyer." "He got lucky, he looks guilty to me, he must have done something wrong, otherwise why would they arrest him?"

Well now, the shoe is on the other foot, your fellow citizens think the same way about you. You have the disease, you have been cuffed, you are no longer one of them, you'll be cast out soon and you'll be forsaken.

You are fighting like a fish out of water you have hired an attorney and spending your money on them. You poor sucker it doesn't matter, the prosecutor has an endless pocket – yours and another two hundred million taxpayers'. The prosecutor does not spare the government's money to defeat you. He doesn't care if you are guilty or innocent he has to send you to prison he has to show a number even if for nothing else but for his own ego. Ultimately please do remember the gift God gave to America: the ability to make money on anything and everything. You are money for the police, the court, the bondsman, the prosecutor, your attorney, the probation officer and the prisons. Without you and suckers like you they would all be out of a job.

Of course you believe your innocence, so you are fighting; you are urging your lawyers on. Naturally they oblige you with a smile they humor you all the way to their banks, they fight for you with tooth and nail especially on the golf course. When you are financially exhausted they'll bring you a 'deal' from the prosecutor which they clinched on the ninth hole. They tell you it is a 'damn good deal' the 'best you'll ever get'. If you refuse they'll take you to trial where they'll throw the book at you and even worst you'll be at the mercy of twelve officially sanctioned vigilantes, twelve morons. You'll be judged by your peers, people you have never met; people who know you only through the indoctrination of the prosecutor. These are people whose life's highlight is your trial, who judge you by their emotion and on their first impression. They think you are guilty since they suffer from the same brainwashed condition that you have had before. "Well he must have done something wrong, why would the police arrest him otherwise?" They also think the prosecutor is there to protect their interest, to safeguard the citizens from criminals like you. Perhaps your thinking was the same when you sat in the jury box before. By the time you realize how 'innocent' you are until proven 'guilty' you are sentenced.

This is the day when even your make belief freedom comes to an end. You are sentenced. You are in a daze, your soul is shattered, you are dumbfounded, and you are speechless. You are still not convinced that you are going to prison you are waiting to wake up from this nightmare soon. Your friends and family are crying. You don't hear them, until the judge tells the bailiff to "take him". The cuffs click on your wrist, you feel the steel, it is cold, it cuts into your flesh. You don't yet make much of it, subconsciously you still think all this is temporary, after all you had a dinner arrangement with your friends and family. They lead you gently out of the courtroom through a side door. You are twisting your neck you are looking back; you still don't believe that you'll be not dinning with them. The side door closes the elegance of the courtroom ceases. Your loved ones and your previous life is behind the door that you may never reopen.

You'll go through few more doors and the scene progressively worsens. Leaving the courtroom there are no more tiles or carpets, two doors removed the walls and floors already dirty and graffiti appears here and there on them. At the end of the corridor are two holding cells facing each other. The bailiff no longer gentle, he opens the door and shoves you into one of them. He slams and locks the door behind you and tells you (he no longer asks you) to put your hands through the bars so he can remove the cuffs from them. You notice a change in his tone he's not as polite as he was in the courtroom. He no longer trusts you, now you are an escape risk, a scumbag. You look around in the cell and indeed you are amongst scumbags. There are assortments of unsavory characters sitting, lying or fooling around in the cell. You are frightened you are different from them. You are still clean, well dressed and clean-shaven. Some of these guys are in prison uniforms some are in unkempt street clothes. What's common about them is that they all scream and yell at the same time. In their communication profanity is a common tread. They may or may not take notice of you and it is better if they don't. In the event any of them ask you what 'you have done', tell them as little you can. However, do not ignore them altogether; by ignoring them you are inviting trouble they don't like you to show that you are better than them. Even if you think otherwise in their eyes you are no longer better than they are. Anyhow just give a brief explanation or an evasive answer. Of course your answer will depend on where you are, what court you have been sentenced at. Generally federal inmates being the 'cream a la cream' will not ask you about your crime, but we'll talk about that later. There are 'only' eighty thousand federal prisoners, all the other incarceration takes place at the state or county level. So there is a greater chance that you are held at the county jail en route to state prison. Each courtroom has holding cells and that is the first step for you and for each sentenced prisoner. Holding cells are only the tip of the iceberg, a mild dose of so to speak on the 'entry level'. The holding cell is a converging point for prisoners coming from different facilities to the same judge. Some of these guys you may never see again, so there is no need to get too cozy with them, but no need to piss them off either, there is no need for them to remember your face. You'll never know where you may end up which inmate you may meet again during your stay in the system. Learn it now in the holding cell and learn it for ever: Don't make waves, don't call attention to yourself, don't be smart, brave and clever, and most of all do not show off and do not make friends. There is no such thing as friends in American prisons. They are all inmates and they all have the capacity to betray you sooner or later. There are some exceptions perhaps in the federal level, but even in the Feds, friendships do not last forever. In county jails and state prisons inmates have no integrity whatsoever; they could and will betray you and even their own mother.

You are still in a shock; you do not believe that you are in there. You are timid you are upset. You don't want to touch anything it might be contaminated. You don't want to be near any of these criminals, you are looking for a corner. The mere sight and smell of the cell and its occupants revolts you. Your stomach is on a roller coaster when some of these guys fart, burp, cough, hack, pick their nose and take a leak or a crap for that matter. While you are in there someone could be doing a number two wiping his butt with his attorney's letter in lieu of toilet paper. There is no partition you are all participating with him, for the others it is natural, for you the end is near. You are still hoping for hope that you are in there by mistake. Every time an officer walks by you are convinced that he is coming to apologize for you being in there. You are disappointed; he is only filling up the cell. You listen to the inmates talking trash because you have no choice. You capture some of the words, but you did not understand their meanings. The stories they tell have no head or tail, they are about inmates and officers. It is a different world and you want none of it. You feel like walking through the wall leaving all of this behind; the inmates, the filth, the bench, the security bars and the toilet. You want to resume your life but you can't. Your legs are getting tired you ease yourself onto the filthy bench. You sit down timidly between two inmates you are afraid to touch them. You make yourself so narrow hoping your clothes don't touch theirs. You think they have leprosy. You start praying. Their clothes match their mouths and they are verbally sparring. They are soon cursing each other over your shoulder; nobody knows why they are fighting. You are the only one who is worried, for the others it is just routine. You hide your face in your hands, you are not religious but you are praying. Suddenly the fight stops, food is passed into the cell. You stay seated; you are not rushing to the bars. You are not yet one of them, you do not fight for the food yet. You get lucky, someone hands you a sandwich. Actually it may have been a sandwich when it was conceived, now it is a flat mess, looks as someone had sat on it. Some cheese and salami embedded in two slices of bread. You don't know what to make of it, a cellophane wrapping just barely holds it together. You may have seen something like this stampeded on at a rock concert. Suddenly you are not hungry; you give it to an inmate across the bench.

Mistake. You should always eat your food in prison. You must never refuse food because of its looks or its smell. Unless you know for sure that the food is off, rotten, or has maggots in it you should close your eyes, your nose and eat it. You never know when you will eat again. The way an army marches on its stomach the same way inmates survive on theirs. Inmates have to be able to stomach a lot of shit looking and shit tasting food. Really it is a matter of digestion; inmates have got to be able to digest shit physically and metaphorically speaking. Elementary as one plus one equals two that physical and mental fitness is the key to your survival – you need both in prison. Therefore, first and foremost you have to feed your body. You also have to realize that you are eating on the prison's schedule. You can not just get up and grab a burger as you used to. You are eating only when they feed you. This is particularly important while you are in limbo, while you are being transported from prison to prison, from county jail to court from county jail to state prison and so on. This is when meals tend to get lost between various shifts and various agencies. Besides, food is the only thing you have left, you are retired from sex, drinks, drugs, and all your virtues and vices. Food is the only 'luxury' you have left. When you get to your permanent camp the food gets somewhat better and more regular, but even there you can end up without your meal. Of course apart from the Feds prison food is always substandard, devoid of vitamins, minerals, nourishment and substance. Most of all – prison food is always inadequate. Therefore you should always eat your food and never refuse it.

Now you are sitting in a cell feeling sorry for yourself your neighbors just started a new fight. This time they promise to kill each other. They snarl, howl and yell next to your ears. You are afraid; you are intimidated, you think you'll be the victim of their fighting process. They totally ignore you yet you feel threatened. You are not used to this, you wish to put an end to their argument, you thinking of calming them down, or call for the officer. Although you are not concerned about them you are very worried about yourself. They did not threaten you; however, you are genuinely terrified of them. You have an urge to shout for help, to yell for an officer. Don't! Just sit tight and do like the others. You see nothing and you hear nothing. Pretend that nothing is happening. It is just routine exercise, just keep out of their way when they jump at each other. Don't ever get involved and don't ever call an officer. Inmates just like spouses, fight for nothing and they hold grudges especially against snitches and peacemakers.

Hours have passed by and you are getting desperate. Nobody has rescued you yet and you think you can not survive this environment. You have had enough time to examine the walls, the floor, the ceiling, the steel bars, the toilet, the filth, and the mess. You even secretly glanced at your cellmates now and then. You are instinctively learning, you refrain from staring and gazing at them. Good thinking. Don't ever stare at an inmate you have never met. Uninvited scrutiny could land you in a fight; they may even think that you are a homosexual. They'll use you, abuse you, they may even kill you even if they are homosexuals themselves.

So far your dignity stopped you from going to the bathroom, but you can hold it no longer. You need to pee badly, but you don't really want to do it in front of them. Unbeknown to you the others don't give a crap, but you have a hang up about peeing in front of them. You fuss and fumble, you turn your back and you are hiding your private part from them. They really don't give a shit about you they are used to shitting and pissing in front of each other. You however, developed a mental block you are standing there with your dick in your hand. You want to pee badly, your bladder is full, you are straining but nothing is coming out. You are having stage fright, you think the others are watching your performance, you are convinced they expecting you to produce a torrent. The more you think of them, the less you have the urge to urinate. You are straining, you are pushing and perspiration runs down your forehead. You are standing there for eternity, you thinking of zipping up in shame without result. Suddenly your mind switches, it takes you out of the cell, you are thinking of your wife, of your girlfriend, the beach, your house, your past, your friends, your urine starts dripping then it gains strength – rejoiced – you empty your bladder. Congratulations, you passed your first test. You see it is mind over matter, you'll be alright as long you don't dwell on your predicament. Of course it is easier said then done; practically your everyday in prison will be a test. Nevertheless just remember with trained and controlled mind your time passes quicker.

Since you went to trial, "they," the system has all your particulars, you may have been nominally arrested after your indictment, or you may have been arrested by the cops dragging you out of your car. You spent a night in jail then bonded out. But before that you have been processed and fingerprinted. That was for initiation only, now you'll be processed for keeps. You are transferred to the county jail. Each counties and cities have their own arrangement but generally most courts and jails are housed in the same complex. This makes sense since they have a symbiotic relationship. Larger metropolitan areas have outgrown this arrangement and have satellite jails as well on their cities' perimeters. In other words you might get walked from the court cell to the jail or might get bussed to a farther place. Both exercises are traumatic but the bus ride is definitely more demanding. Depending on the size of the city/county you are in, it can take anywhere from half and hour to two hours on the bus. You are handcuffed to another inmate, but in some jurisdiction they also shackle your feet. You are still not broken-in, you are still thinking of miracles and even an escape. Don't! Neither does exist. Forget about miracles they passed with Jesus and escaping is even more difficult then his resurrection.

In fact you should pray that the driver gets you to jail safe and quick. You are locked in a metal box with thirty or forty other delinquents, which automatically belittle the horrors of the court cell. Your fellow travelers are all talking, screaming, singing, and yelling. Real jailbirds, you might be the only innocent amongst them. The guy you are shackled with wants to sit, slouch, gesticulate; with every move he literally is 'yanking your chain'. He's got bad breath, rotten teeth, he is screaming to his 'homeboy' two inches from your face. His spit goes into your nostrils, droplets settles on your eyelids. You shudder and you are convinced you just contracted AIDS. Some inmates are chanting and banging on the sidewall although they can see nothing from the outside world. The windows are small, barred up or screened off with non-see through non-breakable glass. The driver and his escort don't give a shit they are isolated from the commotion by a bullet and soundproof partition. The bus may or may not have air-conditioning, you may cook or freeze. The bus may or may not have a toilet facility, which you may think twice of using since you would have to drag your partner with. On longer journeys, let's say to state prisons, the arrangement is somewhat better, you may take a leak. But on short journeys from courts to county jails and vice-versa your comfort is not factored in. If your case is still pending you may take this trip more than once perhaps twenty or thirty times and that's when you should be praying. The more the trips the more chances there are to get into an accident. God forbid a fire breaks out on the bus, or the bus runs into a canal or a bay. Hollywood presents all that as an escape chance, in reality it is nothing but a death trap. If you have ever been in an accident or in a burning car you know how difficult is to get out and away from the wreck. Imagine doing that with a two hundred-pound inmate chained to your hand and legs. The quicker the bus trip is over the better is for you and so you should pray for that.

At the county jail you are herded off the bus, counted like cattle and yelled at. Once inside the 'safety' of the building you get unshackled and processed. The processing could take a few hours or a few days. You get fingerprinted, searched, stripped, catalogued, interviewed, sorted, and screened. Everything is new to you; the building, the guards, their approach, the entire process. You still cling to your dignity; you might even try to talk to the officers. Each guy wearing the guard's uniform seems important to you. You think that one of them could be your savior. You are trying to explain to each that you are innocent. Subconsciously you think that a normal sounding officer is bestowed with a magic wand. Do not waste your breath. These officers do not give a shit; you are only a number to them. Even if they could do something they would not by the virtue of their ignorance. They are simply not interested in your life, in your story, in your predicament. The 'normal' sounding officer might reward you with a reply and tell you to: "Shut the fuck up and get back to the line!"

The 'medical officer' is the least qualified to analyze your ailment so don't waste your time of convincing him or her that you need a special treatment. You should also squash your idea of getting out of your predicament due to terminal illness. You will not be the first or the last to die in prison. The system is well equipped to handle corpses. Your aim is to live beyond prison so concentrate on that.

Remember that county jail is the first step in your calvary; hence it is the worst one. It is worst because everything is new to you: inmates, officers, food, confinement, and the loss of your freedom, the loss of your independence. You are away from family, friends, business and your own environment. And it is worst because as far as prisons are concerned it is the least organized. Here you have different inmates lumped together: sentenced and un-sentenced, young and old, guilty and innocent. Only the facilities are worst than the garbage locked into them. Your biggest problems are the other inmates, the thieves, and the crooks and drug users. Rejects, lowlifes, slime-balls, and every shit you have never imagined had existed. To a certain aspects they are versions of society, creatures that lost or perhaps never had respect or decency. Your biggest challenge is to maneuver amongst them. In county jail you'll seldom find a true criminal, a criminal in the old-fashioned sense, a criminal with 'ethics', 'dignity', the one who became a criminal because he wanted to, the one who still believes in 'honor among thieves'. You might find some of these in the Feds, but in county jail and state prison they seldom exist. In county jails you'll find nothing but society's rejects. Petty criminals, two-bit thugs, drug addicts and ignorant masses; loyalty, respect, decency are all foreign to them. They never had it even when they were on the street. They are totally ignorant about the world, their neighbors and about themselves. They are an uneducated mass, a drug crazed, drug infested generation. They are an insult to the classical criminals to those who are professional in their field and commit crimes purely for business. These county lowlifes have no dignity, no culture, no future, no present, they commit crime perpetually, randomly and often in a drug-induced stupor with no rhyme and reason. They generally range in age from eighteen through thirty-five. These are the ones who cut in front of you anywhere in any line. These are the ones who steal from you and keep you awake, the ones who fight and kill for no reason, who are continually angry and agitated, who have seldom seen their mother and father together and tried every drug by age sixteen. These are the ones you are locked together with; once you survive them you are ready for State and Federal prisons.

Of course the route to federal prison is different; you often escape the county jail in the process. The Feds is a gentlemen's club compared to county jails and state prisons, but I'll elaborate on the Feds later. The road to state prison however leads through county jail and in a sense it is an apprenticeship, a toughening-up process.

So you are in a county jail, you went through fingerprinting and the entire process. You have been assigned to a unit with sixty or eighty others, or perhaps you are in a jail with two-man cells. Which is better? Well, it is six or half a dozen. In a two-man's cell you have more privacy, 'safety', security, and tranquillity. However, most murders in prisons and jails take place in a two-man cell. If you have a good cellmate you are definitely better off in a two-man cell. On the other hand if you end up with a psycho or a clandestine psycho for a cellmate you may not participate in the next headcount.

In a dorm type setting you have 'collectively security'. This doesn't mean that anyone would come to your rescue when another inmate is choking you to death. The collective security lies in the fact that most criminals (unless they are psycho) wish to get away with their crime and without evidence. Of course this is not so easy when eighty other guys are looking on. We are talking about murder of course, out of eighty inmates at least seventy-nine would be willing to testify against anybody in order to get a reduction on their own sentence. The 'snitch-for a better-deal' prevents you from being murdered, but you can still get beaten because in that case the snitch has no incentive to testify, on the contrary the perpetrator remains in the cell to your detriment. But usually in a dorm setting both the beater and the beaten gets moved to separate units after the incident. Keeping a low profile in the dorm environment will help you to avoid a fight. In a two-man cell you can't avoid a psycho while you are in dreamland.

Naturally the dorm life is far from perfect; on the contrary it could be a living hell. Nevertheless it is perfect ground to train your mind to rise above matter. First of all if you are a light sleeper you are in deep trouble. The motto in a dorm: "You sleep when you can not when you want to", or to be more specific "You want quiet go to the Hyatt." The dorm is continuously noisy day and night, sometimes more than at other times. Sixty to eighty inmates run around, scream yell and fight. They have respect for nothing let alone yourself. Simply put, they are worse than caged up animals, they cheat, lie, argue and fight, they don't know anything else, this is their life. Some dorms may have an officer stationed inside, but even with the officer the dorm is never quiet. The guys may sing or play cards next to you or your neighbor plays his transistor radio too loud. If there is no officer in the unit you can forget about sleeping altogether. Even if you are a good sleeper you got to cover your head and ears with a towel. You might still hear the noise coming through your turbine. Don't ever tell inmates to shut up or tell them to be quiet because it is nighttime. You just added fuel to the fire. Remember you are amongst nocturnal animals. These guys don't sleep in the nighttime they seldom ever sleep during daytime. They will annoy you even more or might even punch you in the nose. You better get on with the program; you'll sleep when they sleep if you wish to survive. With time you may condition yourself to ignore their racket. This is another challenge for your 'mind over matter'.

The bathroom is your next frontier. To have cleanliness and privacy, you can forget about that, there are six showers for eighty-four men and only three is working out of that. You may or may not get hot water. You may or may not get into the shower. Even when you do, you'll step gingerly, you are expecting amoebas, amphibians and all kinds of evolutionary creatures to leap at you. It is damp, humid and dark and dirty, it is a real Darwinian experience. To take a leak or empty your bowel, privacy, you can forget that. They may or may not have partitions between the toilets, if you are lucky they may have a four feet high barrier. If you have not lost it yet this is the place where you'll loose your remaining dignity. You'll wipe your ass in the presence of others; you'll inhale each other's farts. You'll have no peace not even on the toilets; inmates take advantage of one another while sitting on the toilet. Forget about doors, this is an open plan. This is a favored spot for inmates to attack one another. Your adversary is vulnerable when he is taking a crap this is when you rush him and stab him in the neck. Three or four sharpened pencils tied together do just fine, your enemy will be confused and literally he won't know his ass from his head.

On quiet days you may end up only being wet from water or perhaps urine thrown by inmate's at each other. It might comfort you that it was not intended for you, well you just happened to be in the crossfire. It is just too bad; it is like a drive-by shooting on the street. What should you do about all of that? Absolutely nothing, unless you are a Mike Tyson or inclined to be an animal yourself, then all rules are off. Are you ready for that? Not just yet, guys who use only brute force to survive they are the ones who keep coming back. There will be time for you to fight, but not just yet, you will learn the signs when to back off and when to fight. But ultimately your survival will depend on your mental strength.

The length of your stay in the county jail seldom depends on yourself. You could be there for a short time or might be there for months on end. If you are already sentenced they may transfer you within a month or perhaps in two or three months. In any case even one day is too much in the county jail; on the other hand if you are still fighting your case you may be there forever. You can not get a bond; you have been in there six months with no trial and no plea deal in sight. You are already on the hook, you took the bait yet you are wiggling, struggling, and flapping your tail. You are wasting your time, wasting your money; you'll never get out of there, at least not without a sentence. After all you are a customer, you got to 'buy or get' something, that has always been the name of the game. You may get frustrated that some habitual criminals get away with their crimes; they will go home quicker than you do. Don't worry the system will get them later, they are return customers. At this moment you are a first time 'buyer', they pay more attention to you, they make more fuss of you since the system wants to turn you into a return customer. With your wrangling and fighting you play into their hands, you'll get a 'special' deal from them. Since you are paying you are the buyer and they are the sellers. Your 'special' deal includes a few years behind bars and ten years probation thereafter. What an after-sale service, they'll make sure that you will always be in their sight. They need you, they love you, and you are their paying customer. In other words even when you are indigent you'll always make money for the system. Smart businessmen in today's America don't put their money into IBM. Forget about Google and high-tech stocks, they don't even bother with them. They invest in prisons and prison related services; through them you are an indentured servant. No, actually not, you are their slave as long you are in the system. What is the definition of free labor that is kept in chains – surely not servant. Cost-free labor, just imagine that. And you and the taxpayers are paying for all of that. It's no wonder that besides businessmen, prominent lawyers and judges are invest in these businesses. Talk about conflict of interest? Of course politicians are never excluded. Their involvement is indirect after all that's why they are called politicians. Legislation, laws and ordinances to suit and protect their investment. Being tough on crime is the best; it is an easy sell. Having been on jury duty yourself surely you know that. The public (and that's used to include you) wants to lock away criminals and that's how it should be under all circumstances. But what has happened lately since the justice system developed itself into a self-perpetuating industry the system creates crimes even when they are not there to begin with.

In Stalin's Soviet Union the KGB used to say "Give us a man and we will fit him with a crime." In America today a reverse theory applies: "Give us a crime and we match it with a suspect." There are countless agencies, organizations in the U.S.A whose existence solely depends on solving (or creating) a crime. How often do you read, hear or if you have not you should have that innocent guys are exonerated based on new evidence, often from death row after twenty, thirty years. The so-called 'Innocence Project' already had exonerated over two hundred and forty-eight cases based on new evidence based on DNA tests. There are thousands of other cases that don't make the news when people get released due to new evidence. These are only the guys who were able to fight for themselves, or somebody fought for them. These are only a small percentage of the innocents.

Don't get me wrong most inmates do belong in prison – I as a former inmate can attest to that. But believe me there is a substantial segment of the prison population that is innocent. Even if that number is only ten percent it still gives you two hundred and fifty thousand people out of two and a half million. There is another half a million inmates whose crime fits the current law book but should have been punished by other means than prison. The law is supposed to be a deterrent, punishing and educating the guilty while rendering justice for the victim. Where is the connection to any of these when the law sends an eighteen-year-old boy to prison for fifteen years for having had consensual sex with his sixteen-year-old girlfriend?

Anyhow the newcomers, the first-timers are the ones that overwhelmingly suffer. The system has a vested interest in them. Attorneys, prosecutors, judges, police and probation officers, counselors, experts, bondsmen, vendors, suppliers and investors all need them. Indeed newcomers, first-timers are the replenishment for the system that employs directly and indirectly hundreds of thousands of citizens.

America has always followed fads and the Justice System is not immune from that. The current "soup de jour" on the menu for the general public and for the prosecutor is corporate crime and sex offenses. Both exist and are real dangers but too often are used as a tool for revenge. I have met a man in state prison who was a well-liked and well-respected football coach in a prominent high school. He kicked a popular boy off the football team for being disruptive. Four weeks later the boy's girlfriend, a cheerleader from the same high school accused the coach of sexual battery on her. The coach, a married man with three children having worked at the school for ten years fought back – believing in his own innocence he took his case to trial. Despite testimonies on his behalf from teachers, parents, students and the school principal he lost at trial. Currently he is serving a twenty-year sentence. How do you comprehend that?

You see dear First-timer your case is not about justice, it is first and foremost about money then ego, revenge, jealousy and personalities. In Nazi Germany people reported their neighbors and enemies to the Gestapo for being communist, in Soviet-Russia to the KGB for not being communist enough. In Afghanistan tribesmen give up one another as Taliban supporters for money and revenge. People are the same everywhere. Americans smear each other with their weapon of choice, corporate corruption or sex offenses. They do this primarily for their ego, jealousy, money or revenge. If you are the accused it doesn't matter. Once the State's prosecutor gets hold of you your situation will worsen. The prosecutor's ego surges, your case goes ahead then culminates in money for everyone except yourself, money for the 'Justice Industry' and eventually for the prosecutor himself. After zealously, ruthlessly and successfully prosecuting you and bunch of others the prosecutor gets promoted, his reputation will soar and he may even get elected into a judgeship or a political office. Besides his ego he ultimately improves his finances and his stature in the community at your expense. It is not about who is guilty or innocent you are an insignificant defender, you are only a number. You are only a statistic to boast with, another notch on his belt. Naturally by the time you get sentenced everybody has made money on you, the court, the judge, the lawyers, the bondsmen, the prosecutor and all the commissary companies. The telephone company and especially your jailers; your own county benefits from your existence. The longer you stay in the county jail, the longer you are their 'guest' the more money they will all make on you, they might even charge you for your up-keeping expenses. Like in a motel or a hotel – in some counties – there is a daily fee for 'staying' at their establishment. They might even charge you for medicine, medical services for seeing a doctor or a dentist. Let's say a fellow inmate breaks your arm – don't be surprised when you get a bill with a hefty fee.

Talking about expenses (which you and other taxpayers indirectly pay for) everytime they transfer you from jail to court and back your State reimburses your county. For example, in the year 2004 Miami-Dade County Jail allegedly received one hundred dollars from the State of Florida for each inmate transported on a thirty-mile round trip from prison to court. In the same time a thirty-mile trip in a Miami taxi would have cost you about sixty dollars.

Anyhow you are sitting in a county jail and you are not broken yet, you still believe you are innocent. You still have some money left; you even hired a new lawyer. You hated your previous lawyer and rightly so. You have been sitting in the county jail close to a year, lately your lawyer had no bedside manners and avoided all your calls. The last time you saw him was three months earlier, he promised you the world yet he could not even get you out on bond. You made a mistake you spoiled his interest when you paid him up front. He is a bigger crook than you can ever be, but you did not know that until he emptied your pockets. You are hoping to recover some of your money from him – forget that. You are pinning your hope on your new lawyer – you are wrong. These lawyers know each other; you are just being pimped around by them. According to your first lawyer you were a 'difficult customer', you refused all the 'good deals' he brought to you. You still believe you are innocent. For your new lawyer however, you are the best customer; he loves you, but behind your back he laughs at your statement when you say: "No matter what it cost I want to prove that I'm innocent."

Well, you are with the pros as far as the cost goes. They'll milk you for everything you have as far as your innocence is concerned you have nothing left. You'll be raped – guaranteed – physically, emotionally and financially speaking unless you can afford to hire Roy Black, Attlee Bailey, Rubin Shapiro or Mark Geragos – without them you do not have a chance. Johnny Cochran is dead, remember American justice is directly proportional with the amount of money you have. Even if your lawyer wins your case and you go free – which seldom happens – justice has not been served when you and your lawyer are aware of the fact that you are not so innocent.

On the other end of the scale there are public defenders, but unless you are dirt poor you don't qualify for them. If you do you'll be in the hands of a twenty-six year old freshly minted lawyer. He is underpaid, overworked, and inexperienced. You may see him only at arraignment and at your trial. They get paid – win or lose – the same. Some inmates never ever see their public defenders, perhaps at sentencing or at the trial. Minorities are especially hard hit, they can seldom afford a private lawyer, in some cases it makes little difference although private attorneys can broker you a 'deal' while public defenders take whatever they given. Don't forget prosecutors and public defenders work for the State for the same master. To put in a nutshell however, unless you are a habitual offender and your life doesn't matter you are still better off with a private lawyer.

Contrary to all of this the Feds are different, as a rule there you should never hire a private lawyer. Public defenders in the Feds are good and much older. They are experienced and most indeed give their best. They have plenty of time to work on your case they are not yet overloaded. Remember there are 'only' eighty thousand federal inmates compared to the two million and plus inmates at the state and county level.

Federal public defenders are also relatively well paid, they generally take interest in your case and they could be as good as private lawyers. However, they do not win cases for you either. Please note and note it well that ninety-eight percent of federal cases end in conviction. Why is that, because if public defenders are good at the Feds the federal prosecutors are even better. They have bigger egos to feed and have much deeper pockets. Their smaller workload also allows them to drag your case out and wear you down like that. They are like bulldogs; once they take a case on they will never let it go. More so in the Feds than in the State if you have taken your case to trial the system hits you harder with everything at its disposal. Most federal cases end in a plea bargain. Hence for reasons above you should never hire a private lawyer in the Feds. Again it is easier said than done, you qualify for a public defender only if you have no assets whatsoever. You'll make a statement under oath that you are penniless, but be careful they can and will charge you with perjury if you mislead them. You see Mr. First-time offender everything leads back to money, they'll fleece you even in the Feds. One more note; the Feds are also quick to freeze your assets regardless of your offense.

Meanwhile back in the county jail you are getting frustrated. The flow of human garbage never ends; thugs, junkies, morons, petty criminals keeps coming and going and you are still there. In the beginning you phoned your friends and family two or three times a day, now they asked you to cut down on the calls because due to you their bill was getting higher. The telephone was your lifeline, through that you still 'lived' on the outside, you wished to know everything and wanted your friends and relatives to sympathize with your suffering and plight. You were making these collect calls at an astronomical price tag; you were the phone company's favorite customer. Do you think authorities allow phone calls from jails and prisons for humanitarian reasons? No, you are a 'captive customer' they want you to make phone calls. The jails, the prisons get a commission on each of your calls. Your friends and relatives have finally seen the light (or rather fainted by the sight of the bill) they stopped accepting your phone calls. You are bitter, you are disappointed. Don't be! They are the ones who are paying the phone bills. Telephone companies charge three times as much for calls from prison; your friends and family can not afford that.

As time goes by deposits into your commissary account is less frequent and might even diminish. Extra food and little luxuries like: coffee, tea, Snickers, deodorant, soap, toothpaste you might have to do without. You might even trade your prison food for postage stamps. You are planning to write a long rumbling letter admonishing your friends, relatives for why they abandoned you. You want to remind them of all the good deeds you have done for them. Please don't. It is time for you to stop 'living' on the street; it is time to accept your fate. Life goes on out there, you have faded. In their place you would have done the same. Although you have not yet been convicted please remember their mind set. In their eyes you were guilty when you were arrested. Most friends – that include girlfriends – last about six months and then they'll leave you altogether. Some diehard friends and family members – if you are lucky – may stick by you longer.

The shitty food is getting to you by now, for Thanksgiving and Christmas you been given compressed turkey slices. You have seen too many fights by now, you have seen blood and guys carried out on stretchers. You go to the exercise yard once or twice a week for an hour to see daylight perhaps a little sunshine. Your health is deteriorating, your gums are bleeding, and you have diarrhea, perhaps constipation. You picked up some skin disease, you are scratching yourself constantly. Scabs and blotches are covering your face. You wait three weeks to get to the clinic they charge you four dollars for a visit. The ointment you are given doesn't help it just makes you sticky. You may be too hot or too cold, there might be A/C in the unit or not at all. You receive a visit, your mother cries, your sister and brother may come the next time. At nights you can seldom sleep. The officers frequently shake down the unit. You have been taken to the courthouse already twenty times. Your new attorney brings you a compromise. You must plead guilty that's the deal otherwise at the trial – when you lose – you'll get twenty years. The judge asks you at the plea agreement "Did anyone coerce you to accept this deal?" "No, your Honor", you reply "Other than the twenty years if I don't sign." The judge frowns and puzzled by you; he leniently gives you three years 'only' and five years probation thereafter. Your new lawyer is happy, he's slapping your back, "I told you I'll get you out of here." Yes, he got you out of the county jail, but before you can go home your detour is another three years via State prison. When he sees that you are not elated he'll offer to appeal your state sentence; for twenty thousand he will give it a shot. When you question him what are your chances for winning he says: "It is fifty/fifty" – well, you would like to tell him: "Go and fuck yourself" but for luck of a better word you settle for "Thank you well done."

Congratulations, you accepted your fate. You are now officially a criminal. Did you notice how your previous world had faded; this time at the court besides your lawyer only your mother was at your side. You are lucky within a month they ship you to a state prison. The bus trip is awful as always, you get chained up like Gulliver from head to toe and in the company of forty others you get bused to a State Reception Center.

CHAPTER 2

State Reception Center (i.e. prison) – Your first step

The State Reception Center despite its upscale name is not a reception center at all. It is not for weddings, it is not for engagements, not for christenings nor for bar mitzvahs. It is a reception center for inmates and criminals like you. This is where you get catalogued, logged, checked, fingerprinted and recorded in every which way into the state prison system. It is a serious exercise, nothing to be snarled at. This is where the D.O.C (Department of Correction) welcomes you into its arms literally and figuratively speaking. Besides the zillions of bureaucratic requirements this is the place where the first serious attempt is made to break your soul. The D.O.C makes an all out effort to indoctrinate you, to mold you into an obedient prisoner. It is a five or six week 'apprenticeship' course it's supposed to prep you for life in state prison. It is like a boot camp wherein you'll learn how to sleep, eat, run, stand, sit, talk, walk, listen and generally behave according to the prison system. Drill sergeant type of officers (prison guards) yell, shout and curse at you constantly calling you all kinds of names and everything under the sun and occasionally they call you inmate Smith or whatever your name is. You are issued with an inmate's uniform and an inmate number will be stamped on all your clothing items, this number will also be stamped into your soul since you'll be compelled to memorize it forever. From this day on your inmate number will follow you everywhere. It will appear on your correspondence, on private and legal mail, as long you are incarcerated this number will accompany your name on everything and everywhere.

In this so called 'reception center' you learn to walk, march, sit, stand, line up or hold hat in hand at the pleasure of a prison guard or any officer. You are to follow orders swiftly, quietly and obediently. You'll also learn to hate them forever, besides the officers whom you equate with imprisonment you'll also begin to hate your fellow prisoners.

I can not emphasize it enough that your fellow inmates are the ones who make prison life harder. Solitary confinement is bad yet some inmates prefer it to the danger, filth, annoyance and betrayal emanating from the other prisoners.

Your journey is immense; perhaps it is endless. If you carry a life sentence you have a one-way ticket; meaning the only way you'll get out is when you are dead. Assuming you are luckier than that and you are only facing a lighter sentence, let's say no more than twenty years. I'm not trying to sound mean by this statement, unfortunately in the United States of America; ten, fifteen or even twenty years is not an unusually heavy sentence. While in other countries, especially in Europe even murderers seldom get more than twenty years, in American prisons thousands of guys are serving twenty-plus year sentences for less than a capital offense. There are judges in America who pride themselves to be millionaires and not in a monetary sense. They are proud of the fact that they dished out more than a million years in accumulated sentences during their judicial carriers. Of course this could be a subject of an other book on it's own, but put it in a nutshell with an industrialized legal system consisting of elected judges, ego driven prosecutors and an antiquated jury system one can not expect anything other than extremely long sentences.

Anyhow assuming that you are a first-timer with a short, long or whatever sentence you'll need to know a couple of things about the prison system you are going to encounter. I am going to elaborate on the most important things, items and subjects with occasional and purposeful overlap between them. The list I present to you is nowhere complete since the American prison system is an extremely complex enterprise. Indeed this list doesn't and can not cover everything. To paraphrase a former inmate who served time in various state and federal institutions: Prison is like a woman's pussy, you can describe it all you want, but unless you have been inside it you'll never really know what it is like. Nevertheless, forewarned equates being forearmed hence knowing about the following will help you while you stay inside. Some subjects I cover intentionally many times, but from different angles. It is done for your benefit, the more you read about them, the better prepared you will be.

In order to prepare you for what to expect on your arrival at a so-called 'Reception Center', herewith I included a portion of my own experience from my previous book titled "Incarcerated":

***

Finally the complex came into sight or whatever Steven could see of it beyond the security screen and the driver's compartment. He could faintly discern the razor wire and the gun tower. The bus idled at the entrance gate for about fifteen minutes before it was let through. "This is where the bullshit starts."-said Ludwig recalling the last time he passed through this center. Ludwig's comment was an understatement, from the moment the inmates got off the bus they were yelled and cursed at. They were herded into a barn type shed with corrugated metal on the side and open at both ends. There were about twelve officers waiting for the prisoners. They were assisted by inmates in blue uniforms with white stripe on the outer edge of their pants. The officers were clad in brown; dark brown boots and pants, light brown polo shirt and dark brown baseball hat. The color may have been scientifically chosen, it was intimidating and brutal. Steven thought of Ernest Rohm and the storm troopers. These officers lived up to that. Gone were the county's "Don't give a shit" attitude and the Federal officers' professional manner. These officers in brown were bullish, thuggish and rough to say the least.

They projected a "No-nonsense, I'll break your fucking bone" attitude from the start. They removed the handcuffs so swiftly and aggressively that it scrapped skin off as well. The red handcuffs were given back to the county officers and the now "freed" prisoners were locked into a fenced enclosure in one corner of the barn.

While the county officers were largely black, the Feds were well diversified, these officers were mostly whites, whites of the small town type. Red hair, freckled faces, blond hair, blue eyes. They appeared to step out of a time gone by with their southern accent and rural twine. They were modern in their outfit however, they all had flashlights, handcuffs, panic buttons, radios on their belts and big shiny badges on their chests. They also had mace on their belts. A short stocky fellow amongst them with a sergeant's rank barked out orders. An inmate in blue uniform hurriedly gave out large brown paperbacks to each newcomer. The newcomers lined up in three rows within the fenced enclosure. The sergeant instructed the group to open up the brown bag and put it on the ground front of themselves in an upright position. Then the inmates been told to place all legal papers, eyeglasses, personal Bibles, Torahs, Korans, up to ten private letters and up to twelve family photos and nothing else inside the bag. Of course all these instructions were yelled out in a military manner emphasizing that anyone not following these orders will face immediate consequences. The other dozen or so officers pacing around joined in to emphasize the threat: "Come' n for fuck sake. Hurry up inmate! Don't bend down! Don't talk! Don't turn your head! Stay in line! Stay behind the fuckin' bag! You, you inmate with the long hair, you have a problem? No, no! you can't keep the fucking comb. Only what you been told goes in the bag. Is anyone here don't speak English? Is anyone here got a fucking hearing problem? What? Where you from…. Oh, from Nicaragua…… How long you have been in America…. What?…. Seven years…… and you don't speak English…… you come to my country and refuse to learn my language, that's disrespect to me, disrespect to my country. Let someone explain to this M.F[1] that he can keep only twelve family pictures…. Twelve, yes twelve no more than twelve for fuck sake."

The prisoners were told to close the bag and place it behind themselves. Then as per next instruction every prisoner had to undress. Undress completely. Standing front of the brown bag and behind their pile of clothes and other belongings the prisoners were given a choice: they could mail their clothes and 'forbidden' items home at a cost or it will be destroyed by the Florida Department of Correction (F.D.O.C.). There were only two guys from the entire group who decided to mail their belongings home. Some guys having been in county jails for months had brought a bunch of stuff with them in their black bags, Steven had nothing to part with, only his federal clothing. After all "contraband" were collected Steven and his group proceeded with the next step.

It was still raining outside; the wind was blowing through the barn from one end to the other. First week in March could still be somewhat cold in Florida especially when the rain is accompanied by a cold front. This happened to be one of those days so Steven and the others were shivering standing there butt naked. Even Ludwig stopped perspiring. Now each man had to upturn the brown bag and dump its content front of their legs. The officers moved from man to man and confiscated any items not supposed to be there. Extra photos, extra letters, additional religious books, pamphlets. Amid yelling and screaming back to the brown bags went the only strictly defined items. Everything else was discarded right into a huge garbage can. Of course the officers wore surgical gloves, they would not touch anything with their bare hands. The sergeant spelt out in his speech that they were aware of the fact that the county jail was riddled with disease.

"We run a clean establishment in here, we don't want any of that shit over here."

He also reassured the group that: "Any piece of shit (i.e.: a human being) comes into this institution will be respected by the officers. You'll respect us then we'll respect you, as simple as that."

"Respect!"-He emphasized- "That's the key word around here. Ya'll respect our rules and we'll respect your existence."

Respect was the theme of the next exercise. Brown bag closed, now officers scrutinized every naked man. They looked into their mouth, ears, and nostrils. They checked hair, armpits, pubic hair, and inspected every scrotum. Prisoners lifted their arms, stuck out their tongues, lifted their balls, blown their noses while officers eagerly observed them. Prisoners were told to shake their heads back and forth then from side to side. Officers rifled through each man's hair, beard and moustache with their gloved fingers. Toes and fingers of each inmate were also checked one by one. For grand finale the inmates had to bend down and open their butt-cheeks with their fingers. The officers took an intense look into that particular depth. To cap it off inmates had to squat and cough simultaneously while pulling their butt-cheeks apart with their hands. No secrets revealed by the cavity, respect duly paid to the officers inmates been rewarded with a red boxer's short. They grabbed their brown bags and marched out of the cage to the other end of the barn.

In their red short but otherwise still naked, brown bag in hand, they lined up front of a glass portioned enclosure. Actually it was an office with serving counters and computers. The group waited outside of this office on the concrete floor for about another thirty minutes. Eventually after another roll-call the officers inside started processing them. Three prisoners were called in at a time for an interview which was rather one sided. Inmates standing front of the counter in red short, bare feet brown bag in hand answered questions for what the officers already knew the answers: "What's your crime? How many times you been arrested? Date of birth? Height? Weight? Marital status? Social Security number?" All that was front of them right in the computer. Some inmates were questioned by immigration officers as well. An officer in civilian clothes – presumedly an INS agent – asked Steven when did he come to the country? When did he become U.S. citizen? Satisfied with the answer he informed Steven that he'll won't be deported. Steven already knew that, and frankly at this stage he no longer cared about that.

After the interview under the supervision of another set of officers an inmate in blue uniform took down the group shoe and clothes sizes. It was evident that all work manual, clerical was done by inmates under the watchful eyes of officers. All skills were vested in the inmates while officers were relegated to the role of a watchman. How economical? thought Steven. It was the same in the barbershop where two officers stood by while an uniformed inmate were cutting the newcomers' hair, beard and moustache. Actually the inmate was neither cutting nor shaping he just simply sheared off all hair from face and head. Each inmate swept up after himself, barefoot in red pants. Right next to the barbershop which was part of the main building the newcomers also received a TB-shot. Naturally all this was under the supervision of the officers. Then back to the barn again to line up for another interview still in red short, bare foot, brown bag in hand. By now a long table was set up in the middle of the barn where the newcomers had to sign bunch of forms as per roll call. They signed for clothing and medical consent and items sent home or kept on deposit with the D.O.C. Steven's U.S. passport the one he was extradited with somehow followed him from the Feds, now it had to be deposited with the Florida D.O.C. Steven signed the form listing his only belongings: A one way, now defunct, useless U.S. passport.

At the long desk the brown bag was emptied and its content was scrutinized again. All newcomers herewith were given a canvas belt with suspender-type of a buckle that locked onto the belt with some teeth. The inmates were also issued with 'bobos'; blue colored flat bottom Chinese moccasins. They were made from cloth-type of material with no heels. Nevertheless a label inside shamelessly claimed shock proof arch and cushioned sole that not surprisingly was non-existent. At the desk the inmates were also given a roll of toilet paper, tooth paste, tooth brush and a bar of soap. The soap had 'P.R.I.D.E' imprinted in it that Steven later learnt that was acronym for Prison Resource-Industry Development Enterprise. On a little sticker – like name tags at convention centers – inmates had their names and D.C. # printed. The sticker went onto the red pants and the same info was written on the brown bag with a permanent marker. Still in red short but no longer bare feet the group was escorted to medical check up. This was inside the main building what incidentally had its doors leading to the barn.

The medical check up consisted of an eye test i.e.: "Do you wear eye-glasses? Yes or no? Cover your right eye, cover your left eye! Read those letters! Okay next!" They also had a sit down interview where a female nurse – old and fat – took their blood pressure then made them sign some forms.

From medical, the group marched to the showers that were next to a supply room where they received a pillowcase stuffed with two tee-shirt, two pair of socks, two boxer-type underpants, two sets of blue uniform (shirts and pants) two bed sheets, a blanket, a jacket and a towel. To be specific that what supposed to be given, however, most of the pillowcases contained only a third of that. Inmates in charge, seasoned and shrewd, reassured the newcomers that the missing items will be issued to them at the compound. Well, that's actually was a lie, these guys were stealing those items and were selling them at the compound. The officers in this case were less than diligent. Well after all, inmates were only cheating each other.

Dressed in blues and freshly shorn the group was herded into a hall. Now they were all Florida inmates officially with numbers and uniforms.

***

CHAPTER 3

Prisons vs. sentences

These two items go hand in hand. You may have started off in a police holding cell, but more than likely upon arrest you were booked into a county jail facility. In America unlike in other countries you are seldom held at police stations for more than twenty-four hours. That is due to the fact that in the U.S.A the justice system is industrialized hence incarceration developed accordingly on all levels. Generally speaking (excluding the military) there are three types of incarceration in the United States.

The first one is the county jail. Every county in America has one. Some are small; others are big, while some metropolitan county jails are gigantic. For example one of the biggest is the Miami-Dade county jail that holds an approximate six or seven thousand inmate at any given day.

Usually the majority of the county jail inmates are un-sentenced individuals who had not yet been convicted. Nevertheless they sit in county jails in some cases as long as two, three or four years. Most states also allow short-timers, guys with short sentences i.e. less than 365 days to be served in a county jail. Other than a short-term sentence or perhaps a minuscule chance to beat the charges the county jail has no advantage over state and federal prisons whatsoever. On the contrary this is the worst of the three since it is always overcrowded, extremely filthy and mismanaged. Here is where you are locked up with the trash, the lowlifes, the scums, the thieves, the dope heads and small time drug peddlers. Generally county jails are revolving doors for urban trash. The county jail has no money, no structure and no program for its inmates whatsoever, it doesn't pretend or attempt to do anything for the inmates' physical or mental betterment. The county jails are simply collection boxes, human warehouses, distribution centers that feeds the insatiable appetite of our industrialized 'justice system'. The only consolation county jails have to offer is that this is where you serve the shortest sentences. A county sentence caps off at 364 days, state prisons take care of anything longer than that.

State prison is a step up from the county jail in every sense. It is more structured, better organized, more disciplined and better supplied. Its facilities are cleaner and less crowded, naturally they have to be since they house inmates with longer sentences. These sentences can run from 365 days to forever. The lock-them-up and throw-the-key-away attitude influenced judges as well; it is not unusual for inmates serving 20, 30 or 40-year sentences. Short sentences like two or three years are rare indeed; the average state sentence runs between five and ten years nowadays.

Perhaps you are a short-timer; your sentence doesn't exceed three years. Nevertheless I would like to call your attention to a very important element in your sentence. If you value your freedom you should guard this with all your senses. It is called 'gain-time' or in layman's terms a sentence reduction for good behavior. Actually it is not a sentence reduction because your sentence will always remain the same. It is a discount on your sentence in exchange for good behavior. It is an incentive and an extremely delicate one.

Most states (and even the Feds) by now have done away or are in the process of doing away with the parole system. In the old days when the inmate had done a certain percentage of his time (50%, 60%, 70% – each state had different requirements) he went in front of the parole board. The parole board examined the inmate's behavioral records (inside and outside) and decided to waive or not to waive the rest of the inmate's sentence. Today there are less and less parole boards and hardly any paroles, instead most states introduced a 'gain-time' system. In state prison each inmate has a work assignment; they all have to perform daily work one way or another. Their work may range from farm labor to library clerk. Assuming the inmate performs his daily assignment and has no disciplinary problems whatsoever he can be awarded with so called gain-time on a monthly basis. The gain-time can be given on a 2, 4, 6, 8 or 10 days of increments. On a three-year sentence with a ten-day monthly gain-time a well-behaved inmate could accumulate

360 days, which is short of five days of an entire year. So theoretically he could shave off a year from his three year sentence. However, according to state law no matter how much gain-time an inmate has, he or she always has to serve out at least 85% of his or her sentence. So if you are the one with the three-year sentence you have to serve at least two and a half years, you can get only a six months discount on your sentence. Nevertheless a gain-time is extremely important since on a ten-year sentence it can give you a year and a half-earlier release. It often can mean life or death.

Naturally very few inmates manage to accumulate all his gain-time since there are a myriad of pitfalls and thousands of ways to lose gain-time. First and foremost you must make sure that previously served county jail time pertaining to your current sentence is credited to you. Most judges are willing to credit you with your jail time, however they do not control the bureaucracy associated with the courts, it often happens that some lazy clerk, a typist, a secretary or an administrator simply forgets to update your record with the judge's order. To reverse their mistake is a nightmare; it can cost you money on lawyers, new hearings, new motions and while sitting in prison that is not going to be easy especially if you have no money. Due to lack of help, due to lack of money lots of inmates in lieu of gain-time end up serving the extra time.

There is another dreaded instrument that can jeopardize your gain-time and that is a 'DR'; it is an acronym for Disciplinary Report. It is a tool in the hands of the guards, the officers. They can write you a DR anytime for anything, anywhere. They can give you one for a sloppily made up bed, for smart mouthing, for back chatting, for fighting or for anything for that matter. Some of the DR's also can send you to the box, which automatically means loss of gain-time. So, guard yourself from being written up. Behave yourself; just bite the bullet, survival in prison often requires more than brute strength. It is called discipline, self-control and mind over matter. Keep a low profile, don't argue, and don't look for a fight, just keep to yourself that is the key to a DR free prison life. Remember you need your gain-time, even if it is only a fifteen-percent discount it gets you home fifteen percent earlier.

If state prison is a step up from county jails than the next level of imprisonment is the Hyatt compared to all the others. I am talking about the Feds. People who have never been to any kind of prison and get locked straight into the Feds may disagree with my statement. Please remember however, that according to the Federal Government we have 'only' eighty thousand federal inmates in the United States. That is barely three or four percent of the inmate population of the entire country. So statistically speaking most of the future inmates will be state prisoners, nevertheless you need to know that better incarceration facilities exist other than the lousy ones you are about to enter. On the other hand future Fed inmates should know how lucky they are that they have been spared from the overcrowded misery of state prisons and county jails.

Anyhow assuming that (the) federal statistics are correct then out of two and a half million incarcerated people only a privileged few, a mere eighty thousand makes it to the Feds. Perhaps because they are less in numbers, perhaps because the Fed inmates are older and different characters or because the Federal Government has more money for its prisons the Feds is the 'cream a la cream' out of all of them.

Just for the uninitiated I must explain that the Feds is not a sequential equivalent of a college or a university in our educational system. Elementary schools, high schools, colleges, universities are logical steps. That's not the way it works in imprisonment. County jail and state prison is not a prerequisite for the Feds. Anybody can get into the Feds without ever completing the previous two steps. Nevertheless by the virtue of our state and federal governance certain crimes just simply don't qualify you to be in the Feds. The everyday murder, thuggery, robbery, wife beating, drug abuse, DUI and thievery belongs to the states. Only certain crimes like cheating the IRS, messing with the US postal service, defrauding Medicaid, and trafficking across state line or international borders in contrabands interests the Feds. Mostly money matters with occasional violent crimes like shooting a US marshal, a border patrol or an INS agent. Immigration violation is also popular with the Feds, illegal immigrants, the smugglers and narco-traficantes ends up in the Feds.

Anyhow for whatever reasons the federal prisons known as the Feds are always cleaner, seldom crowded and always better equipped than the others. Food is better, accommodation is better and the guards are better educated and more civilized than their state or county counterparts.

Physical abuse by guards in the Feds is rare, educational opportunities are more and inmates even get paid for their work in certain facilities (not much of course but at least they get paid).

The flip side of this 'paradise' however, is that sentences in the Feds are always much longer and almost never ever get reversed. The Feds usually prosecute only airtight cases; they seldom engage in hearsay or nilly-willy causes. Unlike in the state system the Feds motivation is primarily punitive and less financial. However, when the Feds prosecute you they prosecute you well, so your chance for appeal is almost non existent. There are thousands of guys in state prisons who are serving time for a crime they did not commit; in the Feds few incarcerated men are innocent.

The Feds' prosecution is so efficient that you'll be wasting your time and money on lawyers. Your lawyer may tell you that he is the best in order to get a hefty fee from you, in practice he is of little help. The Feds win 98% of the cases; do you feel confident that you are that missing two-percent? Just throw yourself at the mercy of the Feds and fire your lawyer. Public defenders in the Feds are just as good as any private lawyer that you can hire.

If you are sitting in the Feds and awaiting extradition to another country, you will not be extradited if you happen to be a US citizen. You will not be extradited - not even for war crimes - for all and any federal crimes you will be serving time here in the good old USA. If you are not a US citizen you will be deported upon completing your sentence, this applies for state and county sentences as well, remember there are enough home grown 'talent' in America they don't need another imported criminal like you.

Talk about 'imported criminals', I should briefly touch on this subject before concluding this chapter. Ingenious businessmen had already figured out a way how to make money on them as well. They managed to turn migrant workers into 'criminal aliens.' Perhaps prompted by certain business interests, lately the U.S. government had stepped up criminal prosecution of illegal immigrants. This automatically provided investors and smart businessmen with plenty of customers: i.e. criminal aliens.

'Criminal aliens,' who are they? Are they creatures from Mars who commit crimes? No, by and large they are Mexicans who cross the border in search of better life. They do what your ancestors did some years, decades or perhaps centuries earlier. They come because the U.S. job market is a magnet. They take a chance in hope of a brighter future for their children. Do you think owners of private prisons that house 'criminal aliens' are unhappy because some Mexicans are on this side of the border? Of course not, they want them to come, they want them to be criminalized – how else would they make a profit on them otherwise. This is the investment that yields the highest profit (45%) for its shareholders. When a Mexican laborer is caught without papers he's no longer deported, instead he gets locked up – often for years – in the so called immigration prison camps. There are illegal immigrants in the Feds as well but most job-seekers who cross the southern borders are held in these private establishments.

These prisons are not run by the states or the Feds – they are managed and practically owned by private corporations. Mostly they proliferate in the southwestern states where financially strapped counties and municipalities are happy to accommodate them. On paper these prisons maybe owned by counties and municipalities although their involvement seldom goes beyond collecting of commission after each prisoner. The lion share of the profit goes to the investors (corporations) who initiated and constructed these institutions.

You see as I said earlier smart businessmen don't waste time with the stock market. They make tremendous profits on 'criminal aliens' while the tab is ultimately picked up by the U.S. taxpayers.

Nevertheless, you need not to fret if you are not an illegal alien, you'll never have anything to do with these places (other than paying for them) but you should know about their existence.

CHAPTER 4

Transportation

I decided to address this important item early since this will be one of the first trials you'll be subjected to on your journey. While in the county jail, while you still think you are innocent, while you still have money and a lawyer to believe in you'll be shuttled back and forth to court often. The frequency of your voyage depends on your case and on your lawyer, but also is influenced by the competency or rather the luck of competency of the court system. On the day of your court appearance you'll be woken at 4 a.m. After being searched, chained and handcuffed you'll be herded onto a bus in company of fifty others. You'll be handcuffed and chained to an other inmate who is not necessarily your friend. You have never seen him before but you already hate him and he hates you back. He however has the upper hand since he's bigger, younger and stronger. He drags on your handcuff whenever he picks his nose, coughs or sneezes; he drags your chained/cuffed hand with his hand even when he scratches his balls or his ass. He may even vomit on you if he suffers from travel sickness. My advice just bite the bullet, it could be worse you could have been chained and cuffed to a psycho who would wrap the chain around your neck with immense pleasure.

The bus you have been sitting on since 4 a.m. is idling waiting for something, you don't know for what and why. It is either too cold on maximum AC or has no AC at all and you are sweating or freezing. The inmates yell and scream to each other, some pray, some sing and some curse. You are lost and intimidated: relax, this is your first trip; you'll have more after this, guaranteed. Try to switch your mind off your predicament, close your eyes and think of something else think of your lover, your wife, your children, and your parents. Think of baseball, football, food, drink, the beach, summer and winter. Do not think of the bus; do not feel sorry for yourself. Do not think of the gorilla you are chained to, just close your eyes and think of something else. Finally the bus starts moving; you may or may not see anything of the outside. Prison buses in America are not designed for sightseeing they don't usually have see-through windows on their sides.

Your hearing is not scheduled till 10 a.m. yet you are at the courthouse by 6 a.m. You are off-loaded like cattle and locked into a corridor or into a holding cell. Naturally you are not alone; you are uncuffed and unchained, for the time being you enjoy the company of the other delinquents. Twenty of you are in a cell designed for ten, no food, no water only a filthy stainless steel shitter in the corner. You getting tougher, you survived this waiting as well. You inhaled farts, coughs, sneezes and stench from the others. Their bickering, arguing made your time go faster. Your hearing is a disaster, in the courtroom you have no friends, no sympathizers. Your lawyer asks you for more money while the court promises you a fair and just sentence. The return trip to the county jail is a reverse matter it tortures you just as well. If you are lucky you are back in your unit by 5 p.m., you are exhausted and collapse onto your filthy bunk bed.

The longer your case drags on the more bus trips you'll be subjected to in the county jail system. Eventually you'll come to the conclusion that the trips are more punishing than the state prison could be. The dreaded bus trips to the court and back torments you frequently, so much so that they influence you to accept a shitty plea deal. The sentence you receive – surprisingly – brings you some relief; you are no longer in limbo, now you know how much time you are facing. One thing is for sure you have had enough of the county jail and you are ready to go to the State. Subconsciously you know the quicker you start your sentence the quicker it will come to an end. Finally they cuff you and shackle you again and load you onto a bus, this time for a longer journey. This will be just as bad but at least for the time being it will be only a one way trip. The bus leaves in the middle of the night – somehow they always do, like authorities wish to hide its contents. Most state prisons are located in rural areas adjacent to farmlands, forests, mountains – so depending on what State you are in you can brace yourself for a long ride. Once again you can not see the outside; you'll be like in a time capsule traveling without any sight. You'll be chained and handcuffed to an other guy. For better or worse for the duration of the trip he'll be your other half. The bus is equipped with a pisser and a shitter but if you ever need to use them you'll do it in tandem with your partner. What? Privacy? I should not even bring it up you have been to the county jail long enough to know that it's nonexistent. Some buses may have a low partition your partner can stand at it's other side, but most have none and believe me it is more practical. It is preferable to see the back of your partner than dragging his arm over the partition so you can wipe your ass. Depending on the size of the State and which of its prisons you are assigned to your trip can range from a few hours up to twelve. You'll get a sandwich or two plus water to hold you over, but if your journey lasts longer than twelve hours you are in Texas or in the Feds. Anyhow the bus will stop many times to drop off and pick up 'passengers'. They all travel in the same class as you are; they are all equipped with chains and handcuffs.

The Feds has prisons in every state so you may end up in Oregon although you got convicted in Miami. In that case you'll fly in a 'private plane' especially outfitted by the Feds for your convenience. Rest assured in lieu of a safety belt you will have enough chains and padlocks to keep you safe and secure during the flight. If you are extradited back to the USA from elsewhere you'll fly on a commercial airline. However you'll be seated in a back seat accompanied at least by two US marshals. Here you'll eat the airline food but your 'safety' still rests with the marshals. You'll be chained, cuffed and leashed up so much that each meal will be a challenge. You'll open and close your mouth while they spoon-feed you since they don't want you to lay your hand not even on a plastic knife. The trip will embarrass the shit out of you since you'll be the boogieman for the other passengers. Any which way transportation for you will always be a torment; you should pray to get to your destination quickly even if you are facing a life sentence. Occupy your mind with everything else while you are transported but do not even for a moment think of an escape. This is real life, this is not Hollywood, a successful escape during transportation is almost impossible and it has only a one in a zillion chance. Remember you are in the hands of an industry that perfected your transportation to a science. I'll elaborate on the futility of this subject later but I can assure you here right now that a successful escape in the U.S.A does not exist.

CHAPTER 5

Classification of prisons

Surely you have watched many Hollywood movies where references are made to maximum-security prisons. The script or the story line hypes up your interest by telling you that the prison you are about to see is especially dangerous hence it is guarded with extra diligence.

Well, in the real reality all prisons are dangerous and all are guarded with due diligence. There is no such thing as low and medium security prison. It is a misnomer; all prisons are maximum security. Gone are the days of Alcatraz, which indeed in its heyday was nothing but a maximum-security fortress. In today's world everything is economically driven and the prison industry is no exception to that. As mentioned earlier, in today's America most prisons are located in rural areas. However these are not prisons in a classical sense they are prison camps, prison complexes. They are like little towns, villages with their dedicated sewer, water, power lines, clinics, hospitals, power plants, generators, roads, streets, storm drains, schools, workshops, baseball, soccer, football fields, basketball courts and all other utilities necessary for their existence. Combined with living quarters, houses, and apartments for the guards, some of these prison complexes rivals in size and population with mid-sized American towns. It is no longer practical nor economical to have a stand-alone maximum-security prison on an island or in the middle of nowhere. Therefore low, medium and maximum-security prisons they are all lumped together within the same complex. So for all practical purposes the overall security arrangements is the same for all of them, with the distinction of having different buildings or compounds within the same complex. While low and medium risk inmates are housed in dorms, high-risk inmates are accommodated in buildings in one-man or two-man cells. During the day inmates mingle at work, at school, at the yard, at the clinic and at the chow hall. They are not separated by background, crime and sentence they just have different sleeping arrangements. During the day a burglar, a forger may work side by side with a rapist, a sadist and a killer. Of course all prisons have high security wings or buildings where badly behaved inmates – some – are permanently locked into solitary confinement.

In other words all prisons are maximum security with little or no chance of ever escaping from them. What sets prisons apart is the amount of perks, 'freedom' granted to inmates within the specific confinement. Some complexes are 'CM' meaning 'closed movement' whereby inmates can move from A to B only when accompanied/supervised by prison guards or officers. In other institutions inmates may move between buildings with a written pass which randomly or frequently checked by roving guards. In some cases all these are waived requiring escorts or passes only from inner to outer yards. But all this rules, regulations are extremely fluid and can be tightened, laxed or removed at the mercy of the warden. So all in all inmates' behavior and management's response to it what makes a prison low, medium or maximum security. From a public's safety point of view however prisons are always maximum security although within the fences inmates' misery fluctuates from minimum to maximum level.

CHAPTER 6

Housing
(Dorm, cell, unit)

Housing is one of the most important elements in prison. This is the place where you are assigned to for sleeping (or lack of it) and for counting. Headcount or counting of prisoners can be as often as five or six times a day hence your bunk bed will be your home for the duration of your stay. Since this is where you'll spend most of your time in prison, housing could affect your existence for the worst or the better. There are two kinds of basic housing with variations on both of them.

The first and most common is a dorm arrangement. It is the most economical from the prison's point of view therefore it is the one used the most often. Dorms are usually A-frame type of sheds or warehouse type of two or three story buildings. They are simple no-frill constructions, yet they are strong and durable. They are equipped with institutional type of doors and windows complete with 'appropriate' bars, locks, screens, chains, etc. Indeed they are well designed to keep you 'safely' inside. All doors are equipped with elaborate locking devices – some mechanical some electrical. Most dorms have vestibules as well consisting of double door-double lock setups. Dorms are usually laid out in barrack formation and often separated from one another by security fences. In addition to each dorms' own fences, the overall dorm compound is also fenced around and separated from the rest of the buildings i.e. chow hall, clinic, library, chapel, workshops, etc. by another fence. The whole prison complex is fenced around again with two additional rows of fences. The fences of course range from fifteen to twenty-five feet in height. They are always substantial constructions; they are not made of chicken wire. Naturally as a rule they are always topped off and reinforced with razor wire especially the outer two fences. Thirty to forty feet wide canals also surround some complexes. Florida prisons also patrolled by alligators living in the adjacent canals. To make sure that you don't tamper with the wires there are strategically positioned observation and gun towers to keep an eye on your movement. The dorms actually are huge rectangular rooms with simple layout inside. They accommodate 40, 50, 60, 70 or whatever number of bunk beds. In one story A-frame buildings the middle of the dorm is usually reserved for single beds in order to enhance the view of the supervising officers. Officers have their own inmate proof cubicle in the center of a two-winged dorm. The cubicles are elevated for a total view. They look over both wings of the dorm. The cubicle is manned by two officers twenty-four seven and equipped with telephones, radios and control panels. Besides the sturdy uncomfortable metal beds the dorm also have a communal shower. Six or eight showers next to each other with no partitions no privacy whatsoever. There are six or eight crappers – institutional style with no lids, no toilet seats on them. You sit on the bare metal or on the bare porcelain. They are separated by three/four feet high partitions just enough to hide your dick or bare ass. The officer however, watches all your movement from his cubicle and will always see your head and shoulders even when you are having a crap.

On your bed besides your sheets and pillow you'll have a wafer thin mattress with one thin blanket for summer and two for winter. It goes without saying your mom is not there so you got to make your own bed. And you got to make it well, there will be daily inspections in the dorm and your bed will be an integral part of that. Don't ever keep any shit under your pillow, in your sheet or in your mattress. Keeping anything in your bedding will earn you an automatic DR. Each bed comes with a metal locker, about the size of a suitcase. You should lock it as soon you can get a lock. You can purchase a cheap padlock at the canteen. It is not much of a protection but keeps temptation at bay. Skilled inmates will open any lock if they want to within seconds. The basic purpose of the locker is to keep certain items out of sight. You should always try to lock your legal and personal correspondence inside. Inmates are abound who steal information from you, personal or legal. They may write to your girlfriend, your wife, your daughter or worse in your legal papers they'll find things which they can and will use against you. Hoping to get reduction on their own sentences they will contact the authorities telling them that you had confessed that you were the second gunmen on the grassy knoll.

That's brings me to my major point about dorms. Other than the shitty accommodation the worst things are your fellow inmates in the dorms. Depending on the size of the building you'll be sharing a dorm with 60, 80, 100 or 120 other delinquents. They will be in all shape, size and color. Their character and age will just be as diversified. They however all have something in common. They are all scums, garbage, and piece of shits. If out of one hundred and twenty you will find one decent (which is less than one percent of the total) you must consider yourself lucky that you are housed in a 'good' dorm.

In the Feds things are somewhat different, dorm-life is more civil, and there are fewer fights, less thievery, less snitches. But as I said earlier only the 'privileged' criminals end up in the Feds.

Anyhow, Feds, county, state and wherever, living in a dorm is not very pleasant. You'll sleep only when you can not when you want to. There is constant noise, yelling, screaming and bickering even after light out. Few officers bother to patrol the dorm for quietness. Don't ever tell the others to shut up because you wish to sleep. The dorm is not only your home but their home too. They will quickly tell you to go and fuck yourself and they might even beat you up. If you can't sleep because of the noise just wrap your head in a towel or create some earplugs. You can make one easily from the spongy part of a flip-flop. You'll be surprised how many things inmates can invent. It is not for nothing the saying goes that necessity is the mother of all inventions. Other than making weapons out of unimaginable things I have seen tattoo-machines made from ball-point pens. In some canteens one can purchase a battery-operated shaver which clever inmates can turn into tattoo-machines using needles and ball-point pens.

If you are tired of a dorm-type of a living you can always break some rules – there are plenty of them. Some infraction might send you to the box where you have guaranteed 'peace and quiet' i.e. solitary confinement. However I don't suggest that. Confinement comes in 30, 60, 90 or 120 days increments. There you shower once a week only and get fed through a hole as they feed dogs in kennels. But your life in the box (SHU in the Feds) is worst than a dog's life in a kennel. You'll be in a tiny cell by yourself no T.V, no books, no letters and no newspapers. You can't see out or over to the other cells. You have no pillow, no sheets, no mattress and no blankets. You'll sleep on the bare bed which is essentially a metal pan built into your cell. You either freeze or fry to death. Even if you survive you'll lose extra pounds – guaranteed. I have seen guys after thirty days in the box losing thirty pounds. The description 'Box' is absolutely apt; it is indeed nothing more than a box that keeps you boxed up in solitary confinement. In the Feds this solitary confinement is called the SHU, it is a wonderful, camouflaged acronym meaning Special Housing Unit. It is special indeed, it is designed to punish you and break your rebellious spirit. The SHU is perhaps the only item from the Feds that is in no way better than its State equivalent i.e. the Box.

Assuming you are lucky not to end up in the box, the other way to have 'private or semi-private' sleeping or housing arrangement is being classified as a dangerous violent criminal. Violent crime/violent criminal, this description is the biggest misnomer in the entire prison system. Theoretically if you physically had hurt, maimed, raped, or killed someone you are a violent criminal and will be punished, classified and housed according to your crime. In reality however all criminals could be violent at any place, anytime even if they have never committed a violent crime. In the same token, a killer may be the most docile person; his crime may have been an aberration due to some unusual circumstance. In other word is not the crime but the individual and his disposition which makes an inmate violent or non-violent.

Anyhow as I mentioned earlier 'violent' and 'non-violent' criminals mingle during the day but for the night they retire into different sleeping arrangements. A one-man and two-man cellblocks or buildings are reserved for the so-called 'violent' criminals. If you happen to be in this classification you'll be sleeping in a one-man or two-man cell. A one-man cell is relatively rare since they are the least economical. If you are lucky to have one it is definitely the best, it is private and safe, you might get bored now and then but you can overcome that by reading, writing, painting, drawing or masturbating by yourself. On the contrary in the two-man cell where most beating, raping, maiming and killing takes place. The chance of getting an amicable cellmate is almost non-existent. Imagine that you are locked together with your wife, with your girlfriend, with your lover or your best friend day after day, night after night in a six by nine cell. You would get tired of any of them after six months. The only time you are apart from your cellmate is when in the chow hall, the clinic, work assignments or at the exercise yard. Assuming your institution has five or six head counts a day you may not spend more than five or six hours away from your cell. (Inmates always get counted next to or on their assigned bed). Imagine having been locked together for eighteen or nineteen hours with your partner. There is absolutely nothing you can do that will go unnoticed by your cellmate. You share every cough, sneeze, fart, noise and silence. You know and see when he takes a leak or a crap. The toilet bowl is wide open there are no partition and no privacy curtain. When he finishes with the toilet, sneezes, coughs, snores, or turns in his bed you'll notice all that, it might even wake you during the night. He might sing, yell, snore all the time; he might have some or no manners whatsoever. He may have hailed from a different background; race, religion, nationality, social status, education and otherwise. He might be stronger, younger, and bigger than you are and indeed he may be a violent criminal. It is just like a marriage, the stronger will dominate the weaker. Guaranteed, sooner or later you will hate each other. Imagine locked together for sixteen hours you will soon hate your wife, girlfriend, lover and best friend, whomever – let alone a lowlife criminal.

All in all you are safer in a dorm; even its bathroom is more private at least it has a low partition between toilets. Sure you can get beaten or killed in the dorm as well but your chances are higher for being murdered in a two-man cell. You might get beaten and raped every night; you might be a 'domestic' partner for a really violent criminal. Guys in the dorms are seldom serving life sentences, even if they are facing twenty/thirty years they are still hoping to get out, by killing you their hope would be gone forever. Some snitch or witness would always testify against them in order to get a sentence reduction for themselves. Your cellmate on the other hand might already be a killer serving a life sentence. He has no chance of ever getting out; he's got nothing to lose by getting rid of you. So the key to survive in a two-man cell – well, you just have to learn to be subservient if you are the weaker man.

CHAPTER 7

Fights

This is the item Hollywood never gets right, in their B.S movies they always present a reason for a fight, they depict inmates as good or bad who tries to reach specific aims through brute strength. Contrary to Hollywood, violence in prison is seldom planned nor is it constant although it is ever present.

Hollywood writers, directors, actors, producers – few have ever experienced prison life. It is like talking about a book you have never read or describing a pussy you have never had. In real prison violence is an enigma. You never know who may start a fight, when and why. You may sit down on a bench in a cell, suddenly an inmate is pounding your head, you have never met him, never seen him before and most of all you gave him no reason whatsoever. You maybe in the chow hall standing in line, a fight breaks, out trays and fists fly, why? Nobody knows not even the guards who watch the inmates with hawk eyes. Do you know why? Because incarceration is unnatural. Caged-up humans are dehumanized, they are like trained beasts they'll obey certain commands, but will snap, bite, kill and fight for no reason whatsoever – when least expected. By virtue of their purpose, design, construction and management prisons automatically ferment violence.

Punishments for crimes were immediate in biblical times: an eye for an eye, a tooth for a tooth had worked and restored morals. An instant justice is more efficient than a prolonged or belated punishment. In America that's what we have an extraordinary long, belated torment and punishment.

So for this and for many unknown reason, whatever, you could be a victim of a prison fight anyplace, anytime. What can you do about it? How can you guard yourself? Not much, but you can minimize it's occurrence by avoidance. I'm repeating the mantra; hunker down, keep a low profile, don't call attention to yourself, don't argue, don't tease, don't brag, don't show off with your past, future or present. Do not tell anyone about your case, don't tell anyone about your family. In prison there are no friends only snitches – so trust no one – your so called 'best friend' can and will betray you at a drop of a hat. America is a nation of snitches – someone always will and can betray you for a deal for himself/herself. In order to avoid fights throughout your prison life herewith some clues you should live by:

Do not discuss, argue, debate, explain or even talk about: religion, race, politics, sports and women. Do not play: cards, chess, checkers and dominoes any games whatsoever, they all generate enemies and will lead to a fight sooner than later. Herewith another example from 'Incarcerated' to illustrate how quickly gambling can turn into a fight:

***

Tony and the heavy set Nicaraguan were gambling regularly just like most other inmates did. Let it be cards, dominoes, basketball or football on TV, these guys always bet on something. In one particular night after drinking some "hootch" both Tony and the Nicaraguan guy got somewhat tipsy. They were not exactly sloshed they would have to drink zillions of gallons of this "home made" brew in order to feel intoxicated. The "hootch" was made of fermented oranges in plastic bottles hidden in the laundry room or under the beds. Cleaned-out empty bleach bottles were obtained from the cleaning crew for this purposes. Squeezed orange juice, pulped oranges, sugar, bread and water were the ingredients. Yeast in the bread served as the catalyzing agent, kick starting the process. Took about two weeks for the concoction to "mature" although inmates often impatiently drunk it before that. It was far from "Courvoisier" but sufficient to dull the senses under the circumstances. It was undoubtedly alcoholic even if it tasted like stale goat piss.

On that particular evening Tony won a bunch of food items from the Nicaraguan. His winning consisted of soups, crackers, Kit-Kat, Tang and items like that. A little while later Tony stopped playing and proceeded to pack away his winning. The Nicaraguan guy followed Tony to his bed where he kept calling Tony names amongst them "chicken-shit". He kept saying to Tony: "Tu eres un pendejo." [2] He also demanded some of the items back claiming that Tony quit the game prematurely. An argument started followed by some pushing and shoving. The Nicaraguan guy pushed Tony sideways and leaned downwards to grab some items from Tony's bed. Tony smaller but leaner immediately hit the Nicaraguan guy with an upper hook. The Nicaraguan shook off the punch and tried to rush Tony, the Nicaraguan was stronger and bigger than Tony, but Tony was a seasoned street fighter. He was also somewhat younger and much more agile. He was also a kind of guy that size would not intimidate him it would just make him madder. He stepped away from his opponent while quickly delivering a couple of punches to his head. The heavy set guy managed to grab Tony but he was more of a wrestler than a fighter. While jerking Tony down to the floor he himself fell in the process. On his way down he knocked the nearby TV set off its stand.

Both of them rolling on the floor Tony recovered quicker, he resumed his blows to his opponent head. Tony was in his early thirties a mid-sized man with muscular physique. His punches packed lots of power and by now were coming down hammer after hammer. He was beating the Nicaraguan's face so quickly and relentlessly that the guy had no chance to recover. He was still grasping Tony's uniform but he hardly put up other resistance. In their struggle they kicked the cable connection off the TV exposing a brass bush protruding from the floor. Due to shoddy installation this brass bush projected upward about three quarter of an inch like a nail from a board.

It made matters worst for the Nicaraguan guy that this bushing happened to be directly under his head after his fall.

Every time Tony delivered a punch this bushing penetrated the back of the Nicaraguan guy's head like a counter punch. Soon he lost consciousness with blood flowing from his ears and the back of his skull. Tony kept battering the guy's head unbeknown to him that each of his blows inflicted double punishment on his opponent. Finally a group of officers arrived, Boreman sheepisly peeking over their shoulder. Two of them escorted Tony out while the others attended to the Nicaraguan guy.

There was not much they could do (or perhaps would do) the guy was flat on his back. He was unconscious and barely alive. He was bleeding from his nose, mouth, ears and the back of his head. The puddle of blood around his head grew steadily bigger. He was heavy, he lay there motionless, the officers contemplated how to put his body on the stretcher. Eventually four officers, one grabbing each leg and arm lifted him onto the stretcher.

A medic arrived from the clinic, who was no doctor just the regular male nurse who usually distributed the daily pills. Neither him, nor the officers seemed in any particular hurry. The 911 urgency what people takes for granted on the outside was conspicuously absent. Neither the medic nor the officers would go near the Nicaraguan guy until they put on their surgical mask and rubber gloves. As they carried out the Nicaraguan guy he looked like a great big orangutan who just been shot with a tranquilizer gun, his two arms dangled lifelessly on both sides of the stretcher.

***

What I'm trying to illustrate with the above episode is that gambling in prison always exacerbate its inherent dangers. So do not gamble or wager on anything with anybody whatsoever. Furthermore do not stare, do not gawk, do not tease, do not pick on or tantalize anyone. Do not be nosy, do not ask too many questions and do not provoke a fight. Do not ask for nor give advice. Do not lend nor borrow anything to or from anyone. Do not join or help anyone in a fight. Peacemakers often end up being beaten themselves.

Ultimately you must remember that in prison someone is always stronger than you are. Even if you won a fight you may lose later when your adversary cuts your throat in the night or stabs you while you are sitting on the crapper. Winners and losers both always get a D.R; surely you don't wish to lose gain-time over a fight.

Fight only when you must and only in self-defense. Aggressors always lose on the end. Prison is full of shifty, slimy back-stabbers and I mean literally speaking. Indeed they can and do stab you in the back or in the neck when it least expected. The reason I keep mentioning the neck because that is your most exposed/vulnerable spot – even when you have your inmate's uniform on. Three No.2 pencils are inmates' favorite weapon – when sharpened and taped together it can end your life quickly when trusted into your throat underneath your jaw.

Fights will occur frequently in dorms, imagine eighty or hundred rats locked in the lab together. Try not to be part of their frenzy, do not get involved, keep a low profile and keep out of their crossfire. Read my refrain again and again: You must keep a low profile that is the key to your survival. Obnoxious, loudmouth, show-off guys – contrary to Hollywood B.S – don't last long in prison.

Most importantly when the fight is over do not give a statement, do not be a witness. Officers as routine will look for witnesses; you were not there, you were deaf, dumb and blind. You were sleeping; you have heard and seen nothing. Most guys come up short when they became witnesses, when they snitch. The state, the police, the prison, the guards, the D.O.C/B.O.P can't protect you from shit. They encourage inmates to snitch but seldom deliver whatever they promised.

Remember you are not a hero, you are not the police and you are not a prison guard. You are not anyone's comrade or brother, just mind your own business, keep a low profile, that's how you survive.

CHAPTER 8

Work

In order to break the 'monotony' of the dorm or the cell – but mostly to keep you out of trouble and make some money for the State or the Feds – you'll be required to work one way or another.

In the Feds you may get compensated (albeit very little) in the State's prison system your chances for payment is almost non-existent. In the Feds inmates work proper shifts in factory-type establishments – naturally entirely within the prison complex. Inmates make: belts, combs, brushes, pillows, blankets, prison or military clothing items, cardboard boxes, paper cups, files and folders. Rumors have it that these factories always turn a profit and judges and attorneys make up the majority of their shareholders.

In state prison inmates hardly ever get paid for their labor although they work on road improvement projects, effluent treatment plants, various public utilities and waste water disposal centers. They seldom work in factory type of environments most of their activities take place in and around their prison complexes. They do work however on lands and farms adjacent to prison complexes. Owners of these farms need not to hire Mexican migrant workers they make far more profit on the inmate laborers.

Most inmates however, are confined to the prison's premises i.e. they are not allowed outside the fences due to their sentences. These guys end up working within the prison complex; in the kitchen, the laundry, the clinic and the library, various workshops and maintenance departments. They do plumbing, painting, roofing, carpentry and all types of maintenance work to upkeep the buildings within the complex. Barbershop and canteen clerking is popular, landscaping, yard and farm work usually given to the young and agile. Agile they need to be especially for yard work, the lawnmowers they cut the grass with are the Flintstone type i.e. they work with manpower.

Inmates are enterprising as ever they make the best of their predicaments. They wheel and deal with everything that goes through their hands. An entire underground economy exist in stolen items: food from the kitchen, clothing from the laundry, medicine from the clinic, bleach/chlorine from the cleaning storage, soap, toothpaste, toilet paper and everything and anything from the canteen by the canteen clerk. Books from the library legal and otherwise – everything has a price. Naturally this is a moneyless society items are bartered and traded including services: a haircut for two packets of soups, a tattoo for a book of stamps.

All work has ranking, standing and status in prison hierarchy. Most are shitty and lowly ranked while others are very much coveted. Working at the clinic or being a library clerk is one of the best, kitchen works; farm labor is one of the shittiest. But whatever work you'll have look upon it as blessing in disguise, it could be worse you could be languishing in solitary confinement, or being bored out of your mind. Whatever your work is it helps to kill time. One of your biggest problems, your greatest adversary in prison is time. You have too much of it on your hand since you are serving a five, ten, fifteen or whatever years sentence. When you have nothing to do or do not know what to do with your time that's when you'll get into trouble, drawn into a fight, start an argument or get a DR. In absence of work in absence of activity your time will drag, stagnate, idle and go slower.

CHAPTER 9

Killing time

By this I don't mean it is time for killing. What I actually meant was that you must find ways to occupy yourself and literally start killing your prison time. Believe me besides keeping a low profile this is the other crucial component of your survival. You should acquire a hobby, a trade, a skill of what you might benefit from long after your release. Naturally you'll learn some manual skills in the prison factory or workshop like bricklaying, welding, carpentry, cabinet making. I'm not talking about these. You need to find some hobby, some activity that you can also do in your dorm, in your cell. Since you'll be spending most of your time in your cell or in your housing unit that's where you have to be involved with something useful to occupy your mind.

The best and easiest is reading or writing. Writing may not be your cup of tea but reading definitely should be. Luckily most prisons – other than county jails – have good libraries and allow you to check out three or four books for a two week period which is ample for an average reader. Remember you can always learn something from books even from the not so good ones. If nothing else they can broaden your vocabulary and improve your grammar. You will not be allowed to checkout newspapers and magazines although numerous kinds are available in the library – you can always subscribe to them if you prefer to read them at your home i.e.: at your bunk bed. With exception of pornography American prisons allow you to subscribe to almost anything – in European prisons you can subscribe to pornography as well. If you have no money or no one on the outside to subscribe to magazines/newspapers on your behalf you can always barter for them with inmates more fortunate than you are. You might even find someone who lends it to you because you hail from the same state, city or just simply because you have blue eyes. By the way all subscriptions, all publications must come directly from publishers or recognized bookstores, you can not receive any kind of publications sent in directly by your girlfriend, family, friends or wife. Once again Europeans are more lenient on this as well; in some European prisons inmates are even allowed to receive food parcels.

If you are not a reader or a writer you can get involved with drawing, sketching and painting. You might be surprised how much talent you have. You can draw landscapes, portraits; you can copy or reproduce postcards and book-covers. You can make cards for Christmas, birthdays, Valentines – the themes are limitless. You can earn a 'good living' by bartering your services. An average pencil portrait can get you a few bags of coffee, tea, sugar, slabs of chocolates, packets of soups, sardines, tunas – all these items may mean nothing to you yet, but in prison they are priceless. (For some strange reason inmates love to have portraits of themselves – since there is no access to a camera or to a copy machine your market is limitless.) In the process you might even discover a lasting talent in yourself; it may even helps you to earn a living once you are back on the outside.

If you have inclination for drawing you can also do tattoos – highly compensated trade in prison especially if you are creative and good with pictures. A word of caution however, tattooing in most prisons is contraband nevertheless it exist and flourishes well.

You can also be a bible scholar. It is the easiest sell. You don't make much with it in prison, the competition is high – every second inmates discovers the gospels upon arriving in prison. It is good to occupy your mind however, and once you return to society you might even end up founding a mega-church. You'll have better credentials than your competition since you have already been to hell and back.

There is not much room for physical exercise in the dorm or in your cell but assuming that your cell-mate or fellow inmates in the dorm don't stop you it is a healthy way to kill time. Push-ups and squats won't cost you anything but they can keep you healthy and occupy you for a while.

Any which way the sooner you'll get into some routine the quicker you'll acquire a skill the better your mind and body will be. Once you fall in love with a hobby you may even find that your time is going too fast and that is exactly what you want.

CHAPTER 10

Chow

The judge who sentenced you made sure that you'll have plenty of time, but he has no control over the amount of food you should be given. Food or chow as it is known in prison will be your favorite subject. While time you will have lots of – food you will always be short of.

The Bible says that man can't live on bread alone – well, sometimes you might have to. Bread is the eternal food and prison authorities know how to spread it from 'A' to 'Z'. They stretch menus to such extent that bread will always supplement your meager breakfast, lunch and dinner. The quality of the bread you'll get is only a tad above shit; it is always the white cotton wool starchy substance. Anyhow, what I'm trying to say is that this so called 'bread' will be ever present in your diet.

Basic pleasures in life are food, drink and sex, in prison you'll only get substitutes for them. While drink and sex are forbidden, food (or its substitute) will be your only indulgence. By law they must feed you three times a day.

The law however doesn't specify how they should feed you and what should they feed you with. In most prisons (other than in the Feds) food vendors, food contractors provide food for inmates and often run the kitchen as well. There is very little control over them; they are usually in cahoots with bureaucrats who signed their contract at the state level. The food you'll eat mostly consist of artificial substances and specifically engineered for institutional purposes. It's cooking and preparation requires no culinary experience. Computer programs tells the kitchen workers how much and what kind of ingredients they have to mix together in order to feed a certain number of prisoners. Real meat is seldom included, once or twice a fortnight perhaps. It comes in the form of hot dogs, drumsticks or junior hamburgers maybe once or twice in a two-week period. Fake meat (tofu, soybean and sawdust) disguised as roast beef or Salisbury steak is given more often. The Salisbury steak even comes with fake grill-marks garnished with plenty of artificial meat sauce. Watered-down grits and oatmeal are breakfast favorites, especially when accompanied by chalk-tasting fake eggs. Fake eggs indeed and they are scrambled well; they are bright orange in color and seasoned well with artificial colorings. Occasionally fruit juice is given although its content is seldom less than 95% water. All in all being a food vendor is a wise investment; the profits are humongous and one never runs out of customers. According to an inmate who had worked as an accountant's aid in the food vendor's offices the cost of feeding an inmate per day does not exceed $2.00.

Regardless of its quantity and quality the chow however, is extremely important. You should never skip a breakfast, lunch or dinner and most importantly you should always eat up everything you are given. Fruit especially apples, oranges – these are the two you usually get – you should eat as much you can. If you are in Florida you may get the latter more often. You can barter your sweets and your desserts for oranges. The dessert is always made with artificial ingredients; oranges however, ward off colds and help your digestion. Please note you can not take food out of the chow hall, but somehow the 'forbidden' food always finds its way to the dorms. It becomes part of the underground economy, you trade, bargain, barter, cheat, connive and fight for it.

Besides your life, food is the other item that you could and should fight for. In the Feds its seldom happens, in state prison now and then, but in county jails it could happen often that some low-life, some S.O.B tries to grab something from your tray. Protecting your food equals self-defense so go ahead use the tray to flatten his head. Even the guards may be lenient and might not lock you up when they see that you were just protecting your chow.

The chow hall is like a stock market; you yell, scream, barter and exchange your food when you can. You might even get a whole tray with its breakfast, lunch or dinner if you find a guy who has sweet-tooth and has cravings for brownies or cornbread. Milk for oatmeal, toasts for grits, a hot dog for rice, a hamburger for a whole tray, four slices of bread for an apple or an orange. In the chow-hall everything is bartered, everything is exchanged. The only thing that puts a damper on this market is when you have a shit-eater, a "come mierda" sergeant in charge as the Latin inmates call a dickhead officer. He is a perverted psychopathic individual who derives immense pleasure from regulating and curtailing your only indulgence.

To underline my point about these perverted officers I include once again a section from my previous book "Incarcerated" It is a word by word description of an actual event that I witnessed myself:

***

There was marathon style feeding, seven to ten minutes given for each meal. Inmates hardly sat down and already they were yelled at: "You have ten minutes, you have nine minutes...... You have five minutes,......You have two minutes...... Time's up. Row one get out......Row two you have three minutes...... You have two minutes," and so on.

The officers at the chow hall were especially mean, they tolerated no delays, they ran the chow hall strictly by their watch. Their time piece may have been calibrated by extra-terrestrials, their ten minutes usually equaled five by any other human being. Just to peel an orange would take at least one minute under normal circumstances. Oranges given at the chow hall were not naval oranges. They were the juicer-kind, their skin was clingy and tight. To peel or cut these, one would need a knife, due to lack of time most inmates left the oranges behind. As a rule, strictly enforced, no food was allowed out of the chow hall. Approximately sixty percent of the oranges were collected and served up again. Inmates called them "relay oranges."

Officers hurrying up the feeding process were lining the food contractor's pocket indirectly but surely. Of course their primary purpose was rather something else: to harass the prisoners. Some perfected the feeding process into an amusement.

A middle aged sergeant, a square jawed one eyed creature had particularly enjoyed the inmates' predicament. He had one real and one fake eye. Like he was out to prove that he can see just as well with one eye nothing had escaped his sight. Inmates regularly traded their food with each other. Milk, juice, bread for sugar or sometimes a whole tray for a pack of cigarette. One night the one eyed sergeant, whom inmates referred to as "Glass Eye" singled out a young black inmate who had gathered some extra potatoes and extra bread on his tray. "Glass Eye," about five feet eleven stood over the inmate and yelled him the "riot act." He cited some paragraphs that forbade food exchange amongst prisoners.

"You have a choice inmate." – He roared – "You have two minutes to eat all this shit on your tray, or I'll write you a fucking DR." The 'DR.' not only meant loosing gain time it could have also sent the inmate to the cooler.

The boy in his early twenties set to work. He dropped his spork and started to shove the food into his mouth with both of his hands. He lifted the tray and slurped up the red beans in one gulp. He rolled up the sliced bread – all five of them – and pushed them down in his throat one after another. "Glass Eye" was standing over him looking at his watch. The other officers chuckled and giggled in the background. All other inmates at the same table cleared out in no time, they handed in their half finished trays at the dishwashing counter. Now it was the black kid racing against time. "One minute," yelled out "Glass Eye." The kid still had his salad, some potatoes and his dessert to handle. The salad was nothing but shredded cabbage, although he accumulated a generous portion of it. The potato supposed to be scalloped potato with some white cream on it. The dessert –luckily this time for the kid – was a slurry looking jelly. The plastic tray was divided into compartments although it served as an "all-in-one" bowl, plate and dispenser. On its right was a groove for utensils but never held anything but a plastic spork and occasional ketchup and mustard. On its middle was a postcard sized trough about three quarter inch deep for the main dish. That's where the kid still had his potatoes. The top of the tray with smaller compartments was designed to hold bread, salad and dessert. The kid grabbed the salad from one of these compartments and like finger food he put it into his mouth in two scoops. His jaws were still busy with the bread mixed up with fragments of beans. The moment he forced the salad into his mouth he also began shoveling the remaining potatoes up, this time with the spork. His arm moved up and down rapidly burying the spork into the food and his mouth alternatively. With his left hand he tilted the tray towards himself to get to the potatoes quicker. The tilt prompted the jelly to spill over coloring the potatoes in the process. His face about to burst, the boy looked like an aggravated puff adder. Below his Adam's apple golf ball sized lumps followed one another as he skipped the chewing process. Just as "Glass Eye" shouted: "Time's up." the boy bent his head over the tray and with one giant suck he vacuumed up the jelly. Debris of potatoes mixed with beans and jelly dribbled down on his chin. "Glass Eye" somewhat amazed with a grin towards his colleagues dismissed the boy by saying: "Get the fuck out of my sight."

This force-feeding was not accidental. It was scientifically designed. It had intended consequences. It did not only line the food contractor's pocket it created immense benefits to the entire department. First and foremost it unequivocally demonstrated who is the boss even at meal times. Its importance to the D.O.C. can not be overstated. It is like training a dog, a lion, a tiger. The subject fears his trainer because beside the whip he can inflict hunger. Fear is good. It goes hand in hand with respect. Contrary to popular belief respect do not stem from love. When someone loves us we take them for granted. Love leads to happiness that breeds contentment then eventually boredom and disenchantment and that's exactly what prison authorities do not want. A bunch of happy, contended, bored prisoners with too much time on their hands. Especially hundred and twenty of them together in the chow hall, next to the kitchen with metal equipments. The plastic trays alone could be used as weapons. So the idea is to keep the inmates on their toes all times. Keep them occupied, keep them moving continuously, constantly with rules and regulations and randomly with petty harassment. That's where officers like "Glass Eye" come in – enjoy going beyond the call of duty. With perversion, sadism, instinctively rather than knowingly they keep the system going.

***

I must warn you that 'Glass-Eye' is not the only stickler, not the only guard who enforces strictly the time allocated to the chow-hall. In most prisons you have to finish your meal in fifteen or twenty minutes. If you get a better officer he may extend your chow time to twenty-five or thirty minutes but don't expect anything longer than that – you are not on a Mediterranean terrace, nor in McDonalds or in Olive Gardens.

As I said repeatedly earlier other than the longer sentences everything else is always better in the Feds. This axiom applies to food and chow-time as well. I can testify that for Thanksgiving we got a giant turkey drumstick for dinner and an entire Cornish hen for lunch at Christmas time. The chow in the Fed is quite ample and not so bland. The allotted time also have a human touch; you always get at least half an hour to finish your meal.

Food of course very much exists outside the chow hall as well. These ingredients mostly come from the canteen or commissary items. Depends on the facility you'll be sent, you either order food from a commissary list or physically stand in line for them at the canteen.

For lack of a better word we call these so called supplements food as well, but remember all these items are highly processed, some are specifically engineered for inmates' indulgence. Honey bun and bear-claw I never had in my life but I learnt to like them and seen inmates trying to kill each other over them. Grain-bars, various nutri-bars, chocolates, candies, cookies, crackers, peanuts, beefjerkies and so-called summer sausages are in abundance. Of course all of these are preserved/ engineered so well that you can keep them in your locker for years and they won't spoil ever. In other words they are devoid of nutrients so much that not even ants, insects, roaches, mold or bacteria would bother to attack them. You can also buy tuna, sardines and diced ham but not in a can, they are packaged (for your safety) in plastic vacuum packs.

All these items they sell to you at exorbitant prices. You often pay three or four times of what these would cost you on the outside at your supermarket. Businessmen should know that running a prison canteen is another excellent investment. You are never short of customers and your profit is three hundred percent. Remember that all you inmates have been convicted of a crime i.e.: you are a criminal. The vendor who is an upright citizen – and often the brother-in law of the warden – goes by the title of 'honest businessman'.

Philosophy aside, (you) beggars can't be choosers. I advise you to eat up your food in the chow-hall – even if your time is limited. Buy wisely in the canteen and don't show off with your riches don't stuff your locker with commissary items. Guys who store too much food in their locker will get robbed sooner or later. Just buy as much you need for a day or two, going to the canteen is an exercise in itself and also helps you to kill time.

By the way one good item from the canteen I can swear by: it is the 'Raman' noodles soup. It comes in various flavors: chicken, Cajun, beef, shrimp and so many others. Soak it in hot water for ten to fifteen minutes; it will produce a good broth. It is good for a sore throat; you can drink it after you have gargled with it. You can make a good stew with its noodles just add tuna/sardines/mayonnaise into it. (You can buy mayonnaise/ketchup in packets at the canteen.) Another excellent dish is once you drink up the broth you can mix pulverized cheetos into the remaining noodles.

If you are one of those unfortunate guys with no money in his account – don't despair, you can always barter your talent, brain, muscle and your services for food supplements. Make a deal with whatever you have but do not go hungry; you'll need your strength. You see, prison is like a giant jigsaw puzzle you'll need to fit in to survive, so learn some skill, a hobby quickly – like that your peace of mind can supplement your healthy body.

CHAPTER 11

Health/Medical

Even if you eat up all your food, even if you eat supplementary snacks, even if you exercise regularly you may still get sick. You could acquire a major disease or end up maimed and handicapped. Barring major diseases you can still get sick and may not be immune from certain prison illnesses.

If you have a pre-existing condition you'll get regular check-ups and medication for that. Once again there is a day and night difference in medical services between state prison and the Feds. In the Feds health-care is almost as good as on the street. Well, as I said earlier there are 'only' eighty thousand federal inmates and the Feds can afford to look after them. Most medical personnel in the Feds are employed by the Federal government. State prisons on the other hand are always overcrowded and always under funded. To compound these problems states outsource and subcontract many services. The medical service is one of them. Companies connected at state capitals usually get the contracts. Just like food supplies to prison this is also a lucrative investment. For this reason – as far you are concerned – the medical service in state prison is a two edged sword. There are procedures, rules and regulations to follow prior to seeing a doctor, prior to getting into the clinic. There are two kinds of illnesses in prison: the fake one and the real one. The clinic sees both of them. They both generate income for the contractor just the same. Back on the street when you wanted to have an extended weekend you asked your doctor to give you a note for Friday, Monday or whatever day you decided to be 'sick'. Naturally you or your insurance company had to pay for the visit. With exception of some county jails medical services in state prisons and in the Feds are free. Free for you since the taxpayers foot the bills. In state prison the medical contractor is more than happy to invoice the State for real and fake illnesses. Therefore you'll always have a chance to go to the clinic with whatever problem you have or pretend to have. So far it is better than on the street. It cost you nothing to go to the clinic. Once there however, and once your inmate number has been processed for invoicing purposes your health doesn't much matter. The profit motives of the contractor kick in and guide you through the 'right' procedures. Nine times out of ten you will not see the doctor. You'll be checked and diagnosed by a nurse or a nurse's assistant. Doctors know well that inmates are good at simulating illnesses. So even when you are sick for real you'll be tarred with the same brush i.e. you'll receive the nurse's treatment. She'll decide on your medication, on your state of health. The prescription naturally bears the doctor's signature; your medical file will contain his notes. The log will show that you've been seen by an M.D. The medication you'll receive is mostly generic and every clinic has a 'wonder cream'. This cream treats everything: eczema, jock itch, athlete foot, sunburn, scabies, insect bites, skin-rash and herpes. For all these and many other things the nurse/the doctor always prescribes the same cream. There is another super medicine the so-called 'cold-pack' that threats everything: cold, flu, cough, sneeze, itchy eyes, runny nose and sore throat, sometimes they work, sometimes they fail.

The dentist is another matter, in the Feds they build you bridges and they fill your cavities. In state prison the tooth-less smile is in, extraction is the most frequent treatment. If you need to self medicate yourself orange peels soaked in hot salty water is good against cold, flu and cough. Vaseline shoved up in your rectum will soften your stool (constipation is a frequent problem in prison). Chewing tobacco will stop your toothache although on the long run your teeth may fall out. Chamomile tea when you gargle with it will take care of your sore throat, drink it and your digestion improves. Washing your eyes with luke-warm chamomile tea cures some eye infections.

I purposely left 'county jail health care' out of my description because it is an oxymoron. In county jails by the time you get to the clinic your body had cured or killed itself in the waiting process. It is so undermanned and under-funded that not even the greediest medical contractor wishes to bid on them. Doctors are interns or has-beens from public hospitals and the nursing staffs are often employees of the county's department of correction. They are nicknamed 'Angels of Death' and I can tell you the description is not far fetched. On one occasion a nurse stabbed my arm with a needle with such a force that it almost came out on the other side. On top of the ineptitude and less than shitty service the county jail still has the balls to send you a medical bill.

All in all county, state, federal the best advice I can give you on health and medical services: just don't get sick! (A note of warning: in some camps you may get a DR for faking illnesses – so use your common sense.)

CHAPTER 12

Clothing & Laundry

These two items go hand in hand. Their importance is not to be underestimated. With clean clothes, clean bedding you can ward of many diseases, you can safeguard yourself from certain ailments.

Laundry service, this is the only thing in prison that deserves a compliment (county jail of course is excluded). State and federal prisons have got this down to a science and in a good way. County jails can not be mentioned in the same breath, their laundry system is shit at best, it spreads more diseases than prevents.

Both in the State and the Feds you'll get a minimum of two sets of uniforms, some camps might even give you three sets. Hats, a pair of boots, winter jackets you only get one each, but tee-shirts, underpants (boxers) and socks you'll get a minimum of five pairs. In the Feds you'll be issued with two towels – big as beach towels and reasonable quality. The State also gives you two towels but they are neither much better nor bigger than dishcloths used in kitchens.

In both prisons: State and Feds, laundry days (at) minimum two – sometimes three times a week. Bedding other than the blankets gets washed once a week. Other then your bedding all your clothing items are marked/stamped or labeled with your prison number. You'll turn in your laundry in a see-through netted laundry bag, which also bears your B.O.P or D.O.C (prison) number. All your whites: socks, tee shirts, towel, underpants get washed and dried in this bag. Outerwear: slacks, shirts, jackets get laundered and pressed separately from your whites and returned to you folded. This of course is not your neighborhood dry-cleaner here everything is done in an industrial scale and manner. Your fellow inmates working in the laundry throw thousands of laundry bags into giant washers and dryers. Your pants and shirts also get pressed and folded by inmates in an industrial manner.

As part of prison rackets 'private' laundry service is available if you're willing to pay extra items to the laundry man. Remember in prison payment means: bartering, exchanging items and services. There is a whole underground economy exists in each prison. Inmates wheel and deal with everything they can lay their hands on. Everything has a price; everything has an equivalent either in items or in services. You can obtain food, clothes, medicine, tobacco, cigarettes, envelopes, stamps; you can purchase drugs or legal services. For a few slabs of chocolates, packs of coffee and other specific commissary items a jailhouse lawyer or a law-library clerk is happy to provide you with legal services. Some are good; others are worthless. You can buy yourself protection or hire some thugs to beat up your enemies. You make the decision what you spend your 'fortune' on, but remember: buyers beware – in prison everyone is a crook, you might end up worst than before.

Anyhow back to the laundry, despite prison you have no reason not to wear clean clothes. Do not be lazy, do not be slack, don't be a slob turn in your dirty laundry as often you can. There are plenty of diseases due to crowding and closed confinement so being clean, wearing clean clothing will be your most important defense (against diseases).

CHAPTER 13

Friends?

In prison your bed is your home, house and apartment. Practically you are wedded to your bunk bed. Besides being your partner your bed is where you read books, magazines, newspapers and also where you write your letters. As (I) mentioned it earlier you should always lock away your letters and your legal correspondence. If you are lucky to have a bottom bunk bed this is where you'll receive your 'friends', your guests. I'm using the word 'friends' in a sarcastic manner. Believe me most of the guys you befriend in prison are not your friends. They are inmates, criminals and acquaintances. You may get lucky; you may defy odds and facts. You may be one of those rare inmates: the one in a million who'll manage(s) to find in prison a true friend.

The majority of your 'friends' however will be users, liars, cheaters, scums, snitches and bullshitters. They'll come in all shapes, forms and sizes, they may have the gift of the gab, they may protect you, they may even care for you for a while, but ultimately if and when they have to choose between you and themselves you'll be the one who is forsaken. Beware of the one who offers you something for nothing: an apple, an orange, soap, toothpaste and a deodorant. If he tells you: it is okay, it is yours for free, it should be a red flag. If you accept it, he'll get it back ten fold, later. There is no such thing as something for nothing in prison. Givers always have an ulterior motive. They lure you in with freebies to begin with, but later they'll make you pay for your naivety dearly. Don't ever take an inmate into your confidence; don't discuss your crime, your case with anyone. The justice system relies – from cradle to grave – on snitches, remember and remember it well: the only way inmates can reduce their sentences if they make deals with the authorities. Your fellow inmates will 'shop' you, trade you, they barter you for a better deal. After two…. five…. ten or fifteen years in the *can* they would betray their own mother in a heartbeat. You may have committed a crime that you have not been charged with, you may have killed and got away with murder, you may have cheated Medicaid or failed to pay your taxes. You may have jaywalked or mistreated your pets, whatever secret you may have you'll be better off keeping it to yourself. Once you share your secret with your 'friend' he'll try to sell it to the authorities to reduce his own sentence. As once I was told by an inmate in the Feds. "We are a nation of snitches my friend." He should know, he was betrayed by his own children. So remember; don't ask, don't tell, but most of all don't ever share your secrets.

There are inmates who can smell your 'wealth'. Your wife, your girlfriend have not forgotten you (yet), they even put some money in your account now and then. Your prison (B.O.P/D.O.C) number is your inmate account number hence anyone on the outside via that number can deposit money into your account. With this money you can buy supplements at the canteen and inmates with no money become your 'friends'. They'll guard you, protect you, accompany you to the canteen and advise you how to shop. In order to cement their friendship to you some may even give you a shopping list. Naturally their friendship is directly proportional with the amount of items they extract from your account. It is addictive, once you start buying for 'friends' it will be difficult to stop them you can seldom wean them without trauma, they might even beat you, blackmail you and might even steal your card if you try to ration them. With a stolen card they can go to the canteen and empty your account before you can report the loss of your card. The canteen clerk an inmate himself – incidentally the biggest crook on the compound – might even be in on the scheme. So don't show off with your wealth, don't tell anyone that you have money on your account. Buy little and buy in moderation – like that you'll keep away the flies and the rodents.

If you are young and not too ugly you might get befriended by an older guy. Keep away from him if he's been in the *can* for a while. Hey may not be gay but likes your company, telltale sign that he is horny when he regularly showers the same time as you do. Showers in dorms are communal your chance of being raped there is minimal. Nevertheless most inmates are homophobic or pretend to be, so if you hang around with an older guy they might label you a homosexual. Anyhow most straight guys don't bother you even if you are homosexual as long as you don't bother them.

There are camps and dorms where homosexuals dominate, you however don't want to be there even if you are gay yourself. Besides the fight for nothing, the fights for bullshit you'll also be exposed to dramatic behaviors that can hurt or murder you just out of jealousy.

You hardly settled in your dorm or into your cell your religious 'friends' already found you and discovered your existence. Out of the many one will eventually zero in on you, he will be the one who wants to save you, the one who tells you what a sinner you are. He will also offer you hope and he'll be very persistent. He seldom wants your coffee, tea, chocolate or any of your commissary items. He'll ask for nothing, he'll ask for no material rewards all he wants at this stage is your attention, your time and your ears to bend. He'll be knowledgeable of the scriptures, the gospels, the Bible, the Koran. Compared to you he'll be enlightened on all the religious and spiritual subjects. He'll seek you out at all times: in the bathrooms, in the showers, in the chow hall and on the exercise yards. He maybe serving a life sentence and waiting for a miracle to happen. He wants you to share his hope and vision and wants you to be his praying partner. Praying and studying the Bible, the Koran is a good way to occupy your mind, however; Luther's doctrine is valid for prisons as well you don't need a middleman to benefit from the gospels. Most guys who discover the Bible only when imprisoned are on a quest for instant forgiveness and redemption. They can become fanatics, zealots in the process to such extent that they may even hurt you if you ignore or question their commitment. It is a historical fact that far more people got killed in the name of religion than by all the criminals throughout the ages.

First time in prison you are like a drowning man. You are lost, you are vulnerable, and you are desperate. You grab onto every straw, a friendly smile and a friendly gesture. Do not kid yourself! Do not be misled! True friends are rare even on the outside yet you are hoping for one in the wilderness. Remember that despite the other inmates you will have to serve your time by yourself. To find a true friend in prison who eases your predicament is like looking for a needle in a haystack. All in all in prison are no friends only fellow inmates who at best leave you alone and don't try to screw you over.

CHAPTER 14

Phone, Letters and the Outside World

Since the day of your arrest your world had collapsed over your head. Even if you were out on bail for a while your life was not what it used to be. Now you are in prison, a convict, an inmate and a felon. Your world now ends at the fence, what remains from the outside are your family, friends and lawyers. These are your only lifelines, your only connections to the outside world. With time moving on you start losing these ones too. First ones to leave you are the lawyers whom you paid so well. While on your payroll they had promised you the moon – now they don't even take your call. You have no more money, you are a spent force and they don't need you they had moved on. Next your friends will wither then fade away. They have their own life to live, you are no longer part of their world and you have already been erased from their cell phones. Perhaps they have not been your friends to begin with they may have been only social acquaintances who latched onto your name, business, boat, house, fame and fortune. With your possession gone they are no longer around. While out on bail some still had talked to you, now that you have been convicted they have no time for you.

Your family now also had shrunk. Remember when thirty to forty of your relatives used to turn up at your house for Christmas, New Year and Thanksgiving or just for a weekend barbecue. They enjoyed the parties, the feast you lavishly provided for them. They enjoyed your boat; they frolicked in your swimming pool. You never asked them for anything you had the wealth, you were popular with them. You were always generous to your relatives, to your nephews, cousins and nieces. Now you don't see any of them. They won't take your calls, they don't reply to your letters and they don't visit you at all. But worst of all your own inner family, your own wife, your own children, your own flesh and blood don't come to see you anymore. Your wife has filed for divorce; she is still too young to be alone. On the other hand your children – just graduated from high school – are old enough to live their own life without you.

So you are heartbroken, desponded, depressed, disappointed and feeling sorry for yourself you may even be contemplating suicide. Snap out of it, bite the bullet, just look around you; it could be worse, you could have been one of these guys, one who carries a life sentence, those who have been given 20, 30 or 40 year sentences. These guys will never again sleep with a woman; these guys will never again eat a steak or taste Kentucky fried chicken. You see someone is always worse off than you are. You with your measly less than ten years of sentence must get into the groove must get into routine. Get yourself a hobby, a skill, a trade, but most importantly you must refocus your mind and stop living on the outside. Don't worry about your wife, girlfriend, children, lawyers, friends, relatives and acquaintances. They don't give a crap about you so stop shedding your tears for them. You have no influence on the outside whatsoever, you can not change their mind nor can be part of their life. (But) what can you do and do well is: start taking care of yourself. You are no longer paying their bills, you are no longer paying the mortgage you are the guest of the taxpayers now, so free yourself from the outside world's burden. Live one day at a time and live it in a low profile. Get involved with a hobby, read, write, learn, study, eat, sleep, exercise and occupy your body and mind.

Your means of communication with the outside world by now is almost non-existent. You have two lifelines left: telephones and letters.

The letters are a simple subject. You write one or not, you'll get a reply to your letter or not. If you have no one on the outside to correspond with, you can always become a pen pal to some lonely woman. You'll be surprised how many are out there who are willing to correspond with incarcerated men. Some as crazy as you are, some are even normal who might even fall in love with you or fall for your gift of gab. Some inmates make a sport of it; they write to many women and they even trade their names and addresses. There are few institutions that may prohibit pen pals but by and large it is a tolerated activity or ignored by authorities at best.

Indeed it is priceless in prison to receive a letter, it is a moral-booster and it is an up-lifter. Regular correspondence with someone will occupy your mind; it can give you hope, a reason to live and an aim in life. Generally letters are encouragements that you have not been forgotten, so don't be shy, correspond with someone; you never know you might even find your sweetheart. Marriage in prison is not unusual; many relations had started as pen pals. On the other end of the spectrum are the shysters (I don't think you are one of them) whose sole purpose is to get money from their pen-pals.

Remember you are in prison so watch what you write; your letter can be censored, intercepted and confiscated. On the other hand your legal mail is supposed to be sacred – nobody can read it or open it other than yourself without your lawyer. You can rest assured however, that prison authorities have already perfected a way to check it for contrabands. All mail gets delivered to your bed that is your home that is your postal address. They usually give it out at the evening headcount. You'll see how much pleasure you'll have when you get a letter.

The telephone is another matter, it can get complicated and it can give you heartache and can even lead you into a fight. Telephones in prisons are not there for your convenience, they were not inspired by altruistic purposes. They simply generate gigantic profit for telephone companies while the prisons get a hefty commission on them. Inmates can make only collect calls from prison hence the recipient pays for them. With desperate inmates telephone companies literally have a captive audience. They often force the call's recipients, friends and relatives of the inmates to keep a large positive balance on their phone accounts. In other words recipients have to pay upfront for the inmates' calls.

Usually two or three phone sets are assigned to a dorm or to a floor in a cell block. Inmates take turns to use them since their hours of operation are limited between 6:00 p.m. to 9:00 p.m. various institutions have various phone rules, but phone availability seldom exceeds three consecutive hours. During these hours inmates can call only pre-approved numbers and each call is limited to fifteen minutes. Inmates are allowed twenty pre-approved numbers in the Feds, in state prison the lists vary from five to ten. County jails have no list whatsoever; you can call anybody with the landline throughout the universe. (Naturally collect calls only). Other than in county jails the phone companies through their computers transmit calls only to pre-approved numbers. Each inmate has a pin code, which has to precede any dialed numbers. After a single fifteen minutes call the inmate has to wait another fifteen minutes before his pin number gets reactivated. The interim allows another inmate to use the telephone. Unfortunately this arrangement exists only in the Feds, in state prisons there is no interim which means an inmate can hog the phone for more than one call. This naturally creates friction, which often leads to a fight.

The worst of course is when your wife, your girlfriend, your children or your lawyer declines to accept your call. That's when some inmates need to be restrained that's when they want to break everything and everyone in sight. That's why you got to accept your fate. That's why you got to stop living on the streets. That's why you got to occupy your mind with something other than the outside.

CHAPTER 15

Escape?!

Forget about it! Your life is not a Hollywood movie. Don't be stupid, stop dreaming about Tinseltown fantasies. In real life a successful escape – meaning when they never again recapture you – does not exist in the United States.

It is quite natural however, that a caged animal or an incarcerated human for that matter has an urge to free himself. Even if you are the one with a shorter sentence there will be time when the idea of escape will cross your mind. Let me elaborate however, why your escape plan should remain only a plan.

First of all please take a good, hard look at your present environment – you'll immediately realize that I'm not talking nonsense. The physical system that has you confined is so well designed, so well organized that your chance for an escape is minimal. Even if you are a superman with a super brain and super physical strength you'll be plotting, going against a system that has perfected imprisonment into a science. Yes Mr. First-timer, incarceration in the United States is an industrialized science. It spares no money, technology, brain and manpower to keep you confined until you have served your time. In other countries you may have a chance to escape from prison because in those countries incarceration is not yet a science, not an industry yet. In every country other than in the United States incarceration is incidental to living, a necessary and often neglected appendage to society. Those countries have loopholes, cracks and deficiencies in their system because they are not yet preoccupied with locking up each and every failed, fallen and misguided citizen. In America incarceration is absolutely perfect, it is a principal industry on par with or perhaps above services like health, education, training, pension and crime prevention. In some American cities, counties and states imprisonment is the mainstay of the local economy. Florida with an approximate fourteen million people already has more than a hundred and ten thousand inmates locked up in its state prisons. This figure does not include county jails which maybe holding another twenty – thirty thousand people. The Sunshine State now not only exports oranges, it also ships inmates to other states. Its over-zealous law enforcement prompted a sad joke: "Come on vacation, leave on probation" – often experienced by unfortunate tourists.

So you see, the prison industry is big and very very sophisticated – you don't have a chance escaping from it. Remember and remember it well that even a failed escape or an escape attempts carries a minimum of five-year additional sentence. In contrast to this some of the other countries also recognize that your urge for freedom is natural hence they don't punish you with extra years just because the guard failed to do his duty.

Anyhow in America you need to be extremely careful about this subject, in some camps even going too close to an outside fence could be deemed as an escape attempt. A trigger happy guard might not let you get close however, he'll just be too happy to pump your arse full of bullets.

Assuming you are indeed superman and despite astronomical odds you have succeeded, your success however will be short lived, it is a given! Don't forget America is a nation of snitches, gung-ho hero wannabees, vigilantes who all want to shoot you, kill you, capture you because they want to feel important. Most Americans are eager to assist your pursuers just to get their two minutes of fame on the TV news at your expense. With the help of an eager-beaver population (about 300 million of them) the juggernaut of the states, the Feds, the police, the F.B.I, the A.T.F, the Secret Service, the Boy Scouts, etc. you'll be recaptured with ease – guaranteed!

To exhaust this subject I'm going to give you another chance. Herewith on your behalf I step into fantasy-land and assume that you have loyal subjects who at enormous cost sprung you out of prison and smuggled you into another country. You think you are safe, you have beaten the system. You may have for a while, a year, two, five or perhaps twenty-five. Unless you live a hermit's life or live in a cave with Bin Laden – one day even if it is many years later (but sooner than later) you will make a mistake. A phone call, a letter, a woman, a new friend, an old acquaintance or a tinniest slip-up on your side can trigger an avalanche. Your pursuers that by now include the Interpol have never given up on you – now they have you in their sight. Once they know where you are it is only a matter of time before you get arrested and extradited. Only less than a handful of countries have no extradition treaty with the U.S.A and even if you are in one of those countries the lack of extradition treaty protects only the citizens of that country but not you. Once you are back in the good old U.S.A you'll be paying through your nose in time and money. Besides the minimum of five extra years for escaping, the court will hit you with additional charges like conspiracy and destroying state or federal property. You also have to pay the extradition cost so even if one day you (may) complete your sentence you are never actually be free. In conclusion: escape in real life is not scripted by Hollywood, it is doomed to fail sooner or later one way or another, so do not even think about it.

Entertainment

Other than being in prison you are not going to have much of the above. Your entertainment will consist mostly of television or your own transistor radio. The radio however, will be a Walkman-type you can listen to it only through your headset. By and large programs on the TV will not be of your choosing; maybe Maury Povich, Jerry Springer, the Young and the Restless, perhaps the local news and lots of sports of course. The sport mostly is football, basketball, occasionally baseball but seldom Ice Hockey. Of course dominance of sport program depends on the state you are locked up in and on the ethnic composition of your dorm or cellblock. The Feds are pretty good with TV-s; they usually provide three large screen TV-s that's mounted high out of inmates' reach. The TV-s in the Feds are set on mute, you control the volume to your own liking through your own head-set which is part of your transistor radio. In state prison regardless of the size of your dorm or unit you will have only one medium size TV. The volume and the channels are controlled by the guards; usually for the taste of the majority, which you may not belong. In state prisons a small TV-room is usually attached to the dorms with six or seven hardwood benches bolted to the floor. In the Feds TV-s are located in designated rec-halls or in large atriums. You can also play cards, dominoes, chess, and checkers in these halls. Once again it shows that even TV-viewing is better in the Feds. If you have money you may buy your own transistor radio, you may barter for it although your ownership of it like that will last only till the first shake-down. In order to prevent radio theft upon purchasing it prison authorities engrave your inmate number into the radio. So if you are in a possession of a radio with an unmatching inmate number a shitty officer sure to write you a DR.

You could also attend church services two or three times a week – it is not really classified as entertainment but you'll be the judge of it. You can sing in the choir, you can join a Bible study group or just enjoy being away from your cell or dorm.

Exercise and all kind of games can entertain you at rec-yard. Football, basketball, soccer, volleyball, baseball (without bats) can be lots of fun. You can also jog, walk, run, you can even do weights (under the supervision of a 'coach' who is essentially a prison guard). Naturally you can also listen to preaching, arguments and even witnesses a fight.

Fights are the main attractions at the rec-yards – sometimes frequently and sometimes only once a day. In most camps fights are on a one on one basis while other camps consist of full-blown gang wars. Since most state prisons are dominated by African-American inmates racially motivated gang fights are less frequent and when they happen their outcome is always one-sided. It goes without saying that black gangs are sure winners in a physical fight. Keep away from gangs; blacks, whites and Latinos they are all bad for your health – just observe their dispute from a distance. Mind your own business even at the rec-yard, be a loner, keep a low profile that's how you survive.

CHAPTER 17

Gambling, Drugs, Sex

I lumped these items together since they share a common element i.e. they are not what you are used to while back on the streets; nevertheless they can be just as detrimental to your health and can extend your stay in the system.

To a certain extent gambling can be considered a hobby, an entertainment that can help to kill time and occupy your mind. However gambling in prison is not Las Vegas it has no docile touch. Here you can not skip town, can not default on your account and can not max out your credit card. In prison you have to pay up instantly or get beaten or shanked immediately. Cheating in a card game is frequent, even chess games are not immune from shysters. The slightest suspicion can lead to a fight and its outcome can be fatal. The stakes are laughable by outside standards but in prison coffee, tea, sugar, postal stamps, a transistor radio is priceless. Moreover, gamblers same as on the outside often gamble just for the adrenaline rush.

Sex in prison (is) indeed the shadow of the real thing. Self-gratification may not even qualify for sex due to lack of privacy. (The guard can look onto you anytime even in a one-man cell.) Masturbation in public – meaning where anyone can see you is a DR offense; 30 to 60 days in the box or in the S.H.U. Having sex with another inmate is the ultimate risk, besides being a forbidden act there are no condoms in prison and the threat of AIDS is ever present.

Drugs. You may raise your eyebrows – drugs in prison, how come? Well, if you are a dopehead don't despair there is enough marijuana in prisons to hold you over for years. Of course it is not gratis. It has its price like everything else and you'll be surprised how competitive it is. Crack, meth, pills also find their way in but by and large marijuana is the most prevalent. How do they get in? I can't tell you (all the details). Rumors have it that most are brought in by the staff. You see the dollar is stronger than sense of duty or righteousness. Your friends, buddies or relatives on the outside take care of certain guards who in turn deliver to you some 'gift' now and then. Visitation halls are ideal for transit especially when the guards' visions are obstructed with Benjamins.

Drug use of course has many perils. First of all you'll be a target for every snitch. You'll be subjected to extra shakedowns by every guard and every dope-head. You might even get beaten or shanked for your stash and definitely be included in every random piss-test. A piss-test is a wake-up call in the middle of the night when the guard kicks you out of bed at 2, 3 or 4:00 a.m. You are escorted to the clinic in company of others where you'll piss in a cup under close visual supervision. A guard actually will watch you to whip out your dick and pass some urine into a cup. If you have stage fright or don't want to give you'll have one hour to produce a piss. Failing to do that you'll be declared guilty and locked into the box for sixty or ninety days. On the other hand if you piss 'dirty' i.e. dope found in your urine you'd get ninety days in the box and forfeit a large chunk of your gain time.

So, put it in a nutshell: sex, drugs, gambling not worth it, after all they are not even the real thing.

CHAPTER 18

Box, S.H.U, Confinement

A few warnings about these subjects; these are all prisons within prisons. You can be locked into solitary confinement for many reasons in county jails, state and federal prisons. You may even get isolated at a clinic or a hospital of any of these institutions. Structured punishment for your behavior however, takes place in the box or in the S.H.U.

The box (sometimes called the hole) is specific to state prisons and as I described it in chapter #6 it is indeed exactly like a box. You'll be kept in there like a dog in the pound: caged, isolated and fed through a slot. You may survive a stint in the box no doubt (although the suicide rate is higher in solitary confinement) but you'll lose weight guaranteed and will forfeit valuable gain time as well. Tours in the box are dished out in 30 days increments: 30, 60, 90 or 120 days with no letters, no TV, no radio, no newspaper, no contact with anyone whatsoever. No one to talk to, nothing to see, nothing to do; you can look at the bare walls, masturbate and shower alone (five minutes max) once a week. Time spent in the box, besides its torment, is more than jerk-off, it is entirely wasted.

The S.H.U (Special Housing Unit) in the Feds is slightly more tolerable, but only in its physical aspects. You also lose gain-time just the same and have the 'luxury' of some reading material and shower twice a week.

S.H.U, box, hole, confinement – all the same – while you in there your fellow inmates will pillage whatever possession you had. So avoid a DR at all cost, you are already in enough shit you don't need to visit the S.H.U and believe me you don't want to go to the box.

CHAPTER 19

Guards, Enemies and 'In-betweens'

These are not synonymous individuals but either of them can make your life a living hell. By and large the number of enemies you make in prison is directly proportional to your behavior. There will always be guys who won't like you no matter what. They don't like you because you snore, cough, sneeze, walk, talk, fart or perhaps the way you look or just because you exist. Fighting, gambling, snitching, stealing, arguing or just showing off, throwing your weight around – on the other hand – can earn you lots of enemies.

You must make a conscious effort not to make any enemies. In the event that you do end up with some you should try to get a transfer out of your unit fast. Low-life shits can harm you while you at sleep even if you beat them regularly during the days. They can also set you up with contrabands or slip some shit into your tea or coffee. They can slide a note – called a kite – under the door of the guards telling them that you have contraband in your bed or in your locker. The guards will shake you down and write you a DR even if you have nothing to hide. There are myriad of ways to harm even the strongest guy, so even if you think that you are superman – someone in prison can always take you down.

While you do have some limited control on how many enemies you accumulate within the inmates you have no control over the guards who I can assure you are not your friends. There are three kinds of guards: the laid-back non-chalant, the paranoid stickler –nitpicker and the macho-pervert.

The laid-back non-chalant type is the best to have. The only problem is that inmates being ungrateful creatures seldom appreciate this kind of officers. They screw it up sooner or later by taking advantage of them and turning them into sticklers. The laid-back officer has a steady home life he just wants his shift to pass with no hassles, no fights. He does the minimum required of him, he doesn't want to fuck with the inmates and he is only there to collect a paycheck.

The paranoid stickler, the nitpicker is the most prevalent officer. He is the guy who follows and enforces every rule no matter how senseless they are. He believes that skipping on regulations can trigger off an avalanche. He is the product of rules and regulations. He believes that being a prison guard is the best job he can ever have. He makes prison his home, his second home and along the inmates he is practically serving his time as well. This guy is happy to write you a DR for every little shit; he believes that life at large consists of inmates and prison guards. He'll write you up for incorrectly making up your bed or having taken your tee shirt off at the rec-yard. You better be in your class 'A' uniform all times, he will not tolerate a missing button, an untucked shirt or a lose belt. Any extra clothing, bed sheets, towels what you may accumulate is a windfall for this DR-happy officer. He believes that all rules and all regulations must be enforced at all cost no matter they make sense or not. He is paranoid about riots, murder and escape; he believes that by skipping a single rule or ignoring a single regulation can lead to all of these. So when he is on duty his paranoia will have an adverse effect on your existence.

The third kind of guard is the macho-pervert guy. He is the one who hides his fear of inmates behind an aggressive façade. He acts as a tough-rough no-nonsense guy, he wish to preempt inmates' aggression by being cruel, crude, nasty and mean to them. He is the one who calls you: shithead, stupid, yo and mother fucker. He is the one who'll provoke a fight with you to lock you up and have a notch on his belt. He will cuff you and escort you to the box personally and gleefully, and once in confinement out of sight be happy to kick you in your ribs or pop you in your stomach. Despite of all his bruteness this is the officer who gets shanked the most often. He is the inmates' mortal enemy; he is the most hated guard.

Besides guards and enemies you'll have to deal with another class of creatures on every floor in every dorm. They are not guards, they are not 'friends' they are inmates legally but their status levitates somewhere in-between of all these. They may have been called capos, foremen in the concentration camps, boss-boys, houseboys during slavery, perhaps skivvies or N.C.O's in certain armies. These are the trustees, the housemen – 'trusted' inmates working in the guards' or prison administration offices. They have the guards' ears and often whisper shit into them. They may snitch or 'drop a dime' on other inmates for revenge or out of jealousy. They are not really snitches in a classical sense. They often befriend newcomers and might even help them now and then. The classical snitch on the other hand is the ultimate coward who will trade any information to better himself. The 'in-betweens' more often than not are lifers i.e.: serving life sentences. Few had retained some integrity while most of them lost it altogether. Although they are inmates themselves sharing a cell, a dorm, a unit with the others – but being too close to the officers – they can not be trusted.

So all in all; guards, enemies and 'in betweens' they can all be detrimental to your health, you should try to avoid them, once again: by not calling attention to yourself.

CHAPTER 20

E.O.S (End of Sentence)

Assuming you read this book carefully and kept a low profile consistently then you might have made it to this chapter figuratively and literally.

E.O.S means: end of sentence, the day you've been waiting for all these months, all these years. You squirreled away your gain-time, you managed not to get a DR. You served eighty-five percent of your sentence; you lost some of your teeth and most of your hair in the process. Your eyesight now is weaker, your mind is duller and you weigh much less (or more since you became diabetic on all those bear-claws and honey buns) any which way you are a changed man.

End of your sentence; you dreamt about this day so often. Finally it is here, you rejoice you think you are free. Not so fast my inmate friend. In the eyes of America you always be a convicted man. You never again can be trusted. Depending on the structure of your sentence you are more than likely will be tested immediately with a work-release program by the State or half-way-house arrangement by the Feds. Both these programs are teasers and essentially work the same. Technically you are still a prisoner but you are given a chance to adjust to the outside world and work within society for a certain period of a time. You'll be housed in a hostel type of establishment in the vicinity of your own city, town and community. You'll be required to work a minimum of forty hours per week and have to buy your own food and rent. You'll have the 'privilege' to wear civilian clothes (no more inmate's uniform) and work among the masses. If you behave and perform your job well you might be rewarded with a furlough for a long weekend. In the meantime the halfway house where you are obliged to stay takes forty percent of your earnings under the pretext of upkeep and lodging. You'll share a room with two or three other delinquents. You are not in prison, but the halfway-house – which incidentally is run by profit driven private companies – has rules and regulations that often are more restrictive than the prison itself. There is cleaning, inspection and roll call just the same. You'll leave for work by 6 a.m. in the morning and return no later than 6 p.m. If you late for work or back they'll write you up. Under no circumstances you can have drugs, alcohol or woman on the premises. While you at work they'll check up on you frequently, they call your workplace three-four times a day, they visit your workplace randomly making sure that you are there.

What kind of work can you do you may ask? Well, work that a convicted felon can be trusted with: cleaning kitchens, washing dishes at fast food places, packing boxes, shoveling shit at factories and warehouses. How do you travel to work and back? You'll walk, run, swim or fly, but more than likely you'll pedal on your bicycle. That's right, your mode of transport will be a bicycle since according to rules you can not take a public transportation nor you can ride in a car. If you break these rules, late to work and back, complain too much or dare to rebel in any manner they just send you back to prison – it is simple as that. Halfway houses are paid by numbers not by success. There are plenty of inmates who can take your place. The State or the Feds will be invoiced the same.

Halfway house and work release is a tease; it is a trap. Smart inmates decline them they would rather finish their remaining time in prison. You had served three, five, ten or whatever number of years now you are out on the street; it is like a candy that you can see or smell but can not taste. With halfway house, with work release you are still on the prison roster, you are still on the chain of the justice system.

Regardless if you skip halfway house or work release you are still on probation after you had finished your sentence. In the Feds probation is mandatory, in the state system probation is not mandated but as courtesy of your prosecutor it is almost always a given. Depending on the structure of your sentence – after you had duly served your time – you still be shackled with three, five or ten years of probation.

You must understand that probation is another diabolical design, it pretends to keep you out of trouble, it pretends to rehabilitate you and adjust you back to society. In reality however it is a tool to ensure that prisons will never be empty since it holds you to a much higher standard than it holds your fellow citizens. I knew an inmate who had a choice of three years prison or ten years of probation. He took the latter offer since he did not want to go to prison. He got tripped up on some technicalities in the ninth year of his probation so he ended up serving the last eighteen months of his probation in prison.

Put it in a nutshell probation is also a trap. In the Feds you are automatically receive a few years of it. It is prescribed in the federal sentencing guidelines. In the state system it's more of a negotiated deal although as mentioned earlier your prosecutor will make sure that you won't be without it. The severity of your probation is usually tied to your offense it can range from six months to fifteen years. As the word implies you are being probed, tested and tried during this time. You might have restriction on your movement; you may have to be at your house before sunset. You may not be allowed to consume any alcohol (drugs are automatically forbidden), you may not travel, may not change address, workplace, phone number without written permission from the court or your probation officer.

The probation officer may intrude into your life at any place for any reason at any time. He owns your arse, you are his bitch and you are there at his pleasure. His word is gospel; he waives more power than the judge, the sheriff and the president. He may be a strickler, a mean dickhead or simply an S.O.B perhaps a crook himself. He can send you back to prison at the drop of a hat. In most cases he is not there to help he can trip you up even with a speeding ticket. At your slightest infraction of the law he can bury you or can vouch for you if he wishes. Anytime you encounter any law enforcement your probation officer must be informed of that. He can help you or he can send you back to jail due to your encounter. A substantial percentage of inmates are in prison because of probation violation. These violations range from real to bizarre or made up offenses.

Probation officers come in all shape, size, race, color, age and gender. While most federal probation officers are decent, state probation officers with few exceptions are megalomaniacs and ego driven. They are the ever present sword over your head. You have to suck up to them twenty four-seven. They are the monsters who have to be pacified and satisfied at all times. Some may like your wife, your girlfriend or may like to get gifts from you at birthdays, Thanksgiving or Christmas time. Some are known to have extracted a price from you for return of good reports on your behalf. Some may look the other way for a price or may even ask you to be part of your action in order not to trip you up. Even if you are squeaky clean and indeed want to walk the straight-line probation officers have a right to come to your home anytime day and night. What if you are having a party or perhaps an intimate evening with your woman? You may lose your cool since he intruded at the wrong time. You'll be his marked man from that day on he can arrest you for hostile aggressive behavior based on one episode. Even if he is a 'nice guy' he can still harass you with a piss-test. He can come to your house and ask you to give urine sample at 3:00 a.m. Do you think he is protecting the public from criminals (like you) or is he just asserting his ego over your arse?

Probation officers also have access to your bank account and all your financial statements. They have a right to ask why and how you bought a flat screen TV or a new stereo. Incidentally you may not purchase anything in excess of five hundred dollars without his approval. He can ask you where did you get all that money and how did you earn it?

If you want to buy or rent a house, an apartment your probation officer must sanction your deal. While on probation you can not own a business nor can you be a businessman. The probation officer however, can and will come to your place of employment. He can talk to your boss, supervisor and co-workers. In other words he can embarrass the shit out of you at any business.

Assuming you went through all these: you have served your time, finished halfway house, paid restitution and completed your probation. Now you are breathing with a sigh, now you think that finally you are a free man. You paid your dues to society you think you are now equal with your fellow citizens: no, never ever, not in America. Forget about the slogan that everybody deserves a second chance. Yes everybody but you. You are a convicted criminal, a felon and a former inmate – you will carry this stigma for the rest of your life. Innocent until proven guilty, equal justice for all, paid his debts to society, everyone deserves a second chance, judged by your own peers, pulling yourself up by your bootstrap, you can be anything you want to, American dream, etc – as far you concerned – they are all fake slogans.

Employment, rental, loan, insurance and most professional license application forms ask you categorically if you ever been convicted of a felony. If you tell them the truth you are automatically rejected, if you keep quiet or lie about your past once found out you'll be fired; your contract will be terminated. (In certain cases they might even charge you with perjury). It seems that our society is designed to support the prison industry. Some communities even wish to have it as part of their economy. Tomson, a small town in Illinois is fighting with tooth and nail to keep their modern prison from closing down. Local and national politicians alike lobby the State and the Federal Government to fully utilize this prison complex in their backyard. According to them the prison would provide employment for three thousand locals. Dick Durbin a US senator from Illinois pleaded on national TV networks (11/16/09) amongst them on NBC and CBS to send the Gitmo detainees to the Tomson's prison complex. On the same day NPR reported on its program 'All Things Considered' that local politicians and citizens lamented that their modern prison was gathering dust. Instead of rejoicing that a prison could have been eliminated they were bitching and moaning like real estate speculators whose investment gone sour. You see with attitude like this and with thousands of new inmates daily coupled with unending recidivism America is the incarceration champion of the world – and for the unforeseeable future sure to retain this spot.

So don't be angry at your probation officer when he trips you up and with the help of a willing judge he'll send you back to prison. Look at it in economic terms – he is only doing his job. He is doing it consciously and subconsciously in such a manner that he is saving it from irrelevance or extinction. His action is reflexive; it is called job security or job preservation. He is only a cog – although a vital one – in a giant system. Please forgive him, it's not only him but all and every member of the 'Justice Industry' relies on your existence. When you f-up you are gifting business to them – without delinquents like you they would all be out of a job.

The nature of a functioning economy dictates that each and every business must look after its own interest. For a business to survive it must nourish, safeguard and enlarge its market. The 'Justice Industry' is no exception to that. You are and million of suckers like you are its mainstay, life-blood and market. Can you really blame them for their effort to have you, to keep you and turn you into a return customer. You see the root of America's incarceration problem is the almighty dollar. Most crimes are money related one way or another. There is a symbiotic relationship between the jailed and the jailer. The justice system is not unhappy when you screw up; it keeps itself going by relying on your greed and misdeeds. Think and think of it logically: if you are a car mechanic aren't you happy to see broken cars at your doorstep. Some you fix, some you partially fix, while others you pretend to fix. You need the return business.

Beyond doubt the 'Justice Industry' is a business and a huge one of it. With its myriad of rules, laws, regulations, ordinances, enforcers and employees (it) makes every attempt to stay in business and flourish.

Nevertheless Mr. First, Second or Third Time Offender the blame ultimately lies with you. Like a careless gazelle that ventured too close to the water hole – you and only you gave the crocodile a chance to grab you.

In conclusion, please remember that once you are in the system you are doomed forever. What can you do about it? Well, just behave yourself and don't go to prison.

CHAPTER 21

Dictionary (jargons, expressions, slang)

Herewith I present you with some words and phrases that may or may not be new to you. However, they are often used in prison and may mean something other than intended by Noah Webster. This list is nowhere complete; it is only a fraction of the new words and prison slang that you may encounter:

P.O.S –   Piece of shit (a despicable, worthless human being).

Outside – anything and everything what is outside of prison.

Inside –   anything and everything what's inside of prisons.

Homeboy – a body, an inmate, a 'friend' or an acquaintance.

Punk –   looked down low-life P.O.S

MF –   mother fucker

Shank –   homemade knife created by inmate's ingenuity practically from anything from papiermache to toothbrush.

<u>Chow</u> – meals (breakfast, lunch and dinner).

<u>Dope</u> – any drugs but mostly marijuana.

<u>Dopehead</u> – a person addicted to marijuana.

<u>The Can, The Box, The Hole</u> – solitary confinement for purpose of punishment, essentially prisons within prisons.

<u>The SHU</u> – Special Housing Unit (Solitary confinement in the Feds)

<u>Shake-down</u> – when officers turn the unit, the cell, your bed or your locker upside down and inside out in search of contraband.

<u>Straight</u> – I am all right, I don't need anything.

<u>Score</u> – can mean a gain, a settlement or revenge.

<u>Shithead</u> – inmates' code for prison guards/officers.

<u>Yo</u> – you, hey you

<u>Bro</u> – brother; a generic inmate address of one and other.

<u>Joint/Can</u> – generic name for all prisons.

<u>D.O.C</u> – Department of Correction (State prison or County Jails)

<u>B.O.P</u> – Bureau of Prisons (Federal agency for administration of federal prisons)

<u>Feds</u> – generic/popular name of all Federal agencies but mostly referring to federal prisons.

<u>The train</u> – consecutive rape of an inmate by multiple inmates (two inmates holds down the victim while the rest of the inmates takes turn one after another).

Lock-down – absolutely no inmates' movement whatsoever, all inmates are confined to their unit, dorm, cell or to their bunk beds.

CM – Closed movement (when inmates are escorted anytime and anywhere by guards).

Headcount – physical counting of inmates (3, 4 or 5 times a day) it is done when all inmates are confined to their bunk beds.

Floor opened – when inmates are allowed to mingle within their unit or dorm.

Floor closed – when inmates are confined to their bunk beds.

Under glass visit – a visit when inmates could see their visitors through a bullet-proof plexy glass only and can communicate with them via a phone only.

Contact visit – a visit when inmates are allowed to hug and mingle with their visitors – naturally under the closed supervision of guards and cameras. It is usually a perk that could be withheld by prison authorities.

Browns – description of guards/officers due to the color of their uniforms.

Blues – description of inmates due to their color of their uniforms.

Dirts – prison SWAT team (clad in black from head to toe) that suppress riots or subdue recalcitrant/aggressive inmates.

<u>Rat/Snitch</u> – a low-life piece of shit who betrays other inmates.

<u>Dawg</u> – black inmates' slang with various meanings but mostly: body/brother.

<u>C.O</u> – Correction Officer/Prison Guard.

<u>Bitch</u> – synonymous with dick head, shit head, dip shit, etc.

<u>Down</u> – the state of being incarcerated usually with reference to the number of years one has been locked up.

<u>Punk-ass-bitch</u> – Worthless piece of shit, someone, who should be beaten, raped, humiliated and generally taught a lesson by physical punishment.

<u>Nigger</u> – only black inmates have a right to use this word – it is more like a term of endearment and less of an insult when used by black inmates. African American inmates often refer to each other with this word and most times in a friendly manner.

<u>Respect</u> – this is a major issue in prison; it is constantly cited, demanded and referred to by both inmates and officers. It is however extremely elusive, nobody ever gets it, yet inmates are willing to kill for it. Officers perpetually look for it and beat you up or lock you up if you fail to deliver it.

ENDNOTES

1   M.F. – 'Mother Fucker' – commonly used in American street language.
2   'Tu eres un pendejo' – Literally it means: "You are a pubic hair." However, in Spanish slang it is a serious insult meaning "you have no balls, you are chicken shit."